Love & Friendship Samplers

Sharon Perna

Sterling Publishing Co., Inc.   New York

In memory of Isadora and Roy Arlington Hopper—my wonderfully unique grandparents, whose abundant love and affection will always remain deep within my heart.

Edited by Barbara Busch

Library of Congress Cataloging-in-Publication Data

Perna, Sharon.
    Love & friendship samplers / Sharon Perna.
        p.   cm.
    Includes index.
    ISBN 0-8069-6738-2
        1. Cross-stitch—Patterns.   2. Samplers.   3. Mottoes.   I. Title.
II. Title: Love and friendship samplers.
TT778.C76P43 1988
746.44—dc 19
                                                                87-25553
                                                                CIP

1 3 5 7 9 10 8 6 4 2

Copyright ©1988 by Sharon Perna
Published by Sterling Publishing Co., Inc.
Two Park Avenue, New York, N.Y. 10016
Distributed in Canada by Oak Tree Press Ltd.
% Canadian Manda Group, P. O. Box 920, Station U
Toronto, Ontario, Canada M8Z 5P9
Distributed in the United Kingdom by Blandford Press
Link House, West Street, Poole, Dorset BH15 1LL, England
Distributed in Australia by Capricorn Ltd.
P. O. Box 665, Lane Cove, NSW 2066
Manufactured in the United States of America

Contents

Color Section follows page 32

Introduction

When I started the needlework for this book, it was my aim to create a cross-stitch collection of 34 designs featuring a heart motif. Since the heart is the symbol of our desires and affections, I wanted the designs to reflect love, caring, friendship, and sharing. Within this format I grouped the needlework into four categories. In the "Heart and House" section, nine designs combine a heart, a house, and often a well-known verse. The projects here are suitable for a variety of rooms in your home.

In the second segment entitled "Gifts of Love and Friendship," there are eleven items to make for special loved ones and friends. Often these articles are personal in nature—things like bookmarks, bags, a belt, or a photo album cover.

In "Love and Romance," seven presents are featured for the bride-to-be. These patterns carry good wishes and mix names, ribbons, ruffles, and lace.

And finally, in "Words of Love," seven samplers incorporate timeless and enduring quotations that define love at its best. These quotations come from such sources as the Bible, playwrights, poets, and songs.

As for the designs in this assembly, several styles are represented. Some are very realistic, others are stylized and abstracted, and there are those that have been turned into geometric repeats. During the planning stages of these styles, I also tried to combine different embroidery palettes, an assortment of fabrics and counts, and an interesting variety of sampler motifs. But most of all I wanted you to have the experience of creating a beautifully stitched object that served a practical purpose as well. Hopefully, I joined all these elements harmoniously to please your eyes, hands, and heart.

METRIC EQUIVALENCY CHART

MM—MILLIMETRES   CM—CENTIMETRES

INCHES TO MILLIMETRES AND CENTIMETRES

INCHES	MM	CM	INCHES	CM	INCHES	CM
⅛	3	0.3	9	22.9	30	76.2
¼	6	0.6	10	25.4	31	78.7
⅜	10	1.0	11	27.9	32	81.3
½	13	1.3	12	30.5	33	83.8
⅝	16	1.6	13	33.0	34	86.4
¾	19	1.9	14	35.6	35	88.9
⅞	22	2.2	15	38.1	36	91.4
1	25	2.5	16	40.6	37	94.0
1¼	32	3.2	17	43.2	38	96.5
1½	38	3.8	18	45.7	39	99.1
1¾	44	4.4	19	48.3	40	101.6
2	51	5.1	20	50.8	41	104.1
2½	64	6.4	21	53.3	42	106.7
3	76	7.6	22	55.9	43	109.2
3½	89	8.9	23	58.4	44	111.8
4	102	10.2	24	61.0	45	114.3
4½	114	11.4	25	63.5	46	116.8
5	127	12.7	26	66.0	47	119.4
6	152	15.2	27	68.6	48	121.9
7	178	17.8	28	71.1	49	124.5
8	203	20.3	29	73.7	50	127.0

YARDS TO METRES

YARDS	METRES	YARDS	METRES	YARDS	METRES	YARDS	METRES	YARDS	METRES
⅛	0.11	2⅛	1.94	4⅛	3.77	6⅛	5.60	8⅛	7.43
¼	0.23	2¼	2.06	4¼	3.89	6¼	5.72	8¼	7.54
⅜	0.34	2⅜	2.17	4⅜	4.00	6⅜	5.83	8⅜	7.66
½	0.46	2½	2.29	4½	4.11	6½	5.94	8½	7.77
⅝	0.57	2⅝	2.40	4⅝	4.23	6⅝	6.06	8⅝	7.89
¾	0.69	2¾	2.51	4¾	4.34	6¾	6.17	8¾	8.00
⅞	0.80	2⅞	2.63	4⅞	4.46	6⅞	6.29	8⅞	8.12
1	0.91	3	2.74	5	4.57	7	6.40	9	8.23
1⅛	1.03	3⅛	2.86	5⅛	4.69	7⅛	6.52	9⅛	8.34
1¼	1.14	3¼	2.97	5¼	4.80	7¼	6.63	9¼	8.46
1⅜	1.26	3⅜	3.09	5⅜	4.91	7⅜	6.74	9⅜	8.57
1½	1.37	3½	3.20	5½	5.03	7½	6.86	9½	8.69
1⅝	1.49	3⅝	3.31	5⅝	5.14	7⅝	6.97	9⅝	8.80
1¾	1.60	3¾	3.43	5¾	5.26	7¾	7.09	9¾	8.92
1⅞	1.71	3⅞	3.54	5⅞	5.37	7⅞	7.20	9⅞	9.03
2	1.83	4	3.66	6	5.49	8	7.32	10	9.14

MATERIALS AND TECHNIQUES

Materials

The Fabrics

Cross-stitching is done on an evenweave fabric of cotton or linen. Evenweave means that the fabric has approximately the same number of threads to the inch in both directions of the cloth (horizontally and vertically). Just as the textile you will embroider has a natural woven grid, the charted graph you will work from also has a corresponding framework.

Aida is a 100% cotton fabric available in white, ivory, solid colors, and in two and multicolor combinations. It is usually sold in precut pieces measuring 12″ × 18″, 15″ × 15″, 18″ × 30″, 36″ × 60″ (1-yard packages), or in bolts of 60-inch widths. The count of the fabric, that is, the number of cross-stitches you can sew in a one-inch space (Illus. 1), is either 8, 11, 14, or 18. You should also understand that the fabric count can be expressed in different ways, but the interpretation is always the same. For example #8 aida, aida 8, 8-count aida cloth, and 8/1″ all mean you can embroider 8 cross-stitches per inch on that particular fabric. If a project calls for a specific count, that is the cloth you

should buy. Using another count only alters and distorts the final appearance of the design.

Pure linen is an elegant, traditional, and durable fabric. We tend to associate it with European embroiderers, but this is the cloth from which heirlooms are made. Linen comes in white (bleached), shades of ivory (unbleached), and a few pastel colors. It is usually sold by the yard in bolts that are approximately 52″ to 57″ wide. The most popular thread counts are 12, 18, 19, 20, 24, 27, and 30 threads per inch. Since cross- and back-stitches are stitched over two threads on linen, a thread count of, for example, 20 is really 10 cross-stitches per inch. It is also important to understand that as the thread count increases, the linen, obviously, becomes finer, tighter, and softer to the touch.

There are three things you need to learn about evenweave fabrics: The cotton or linen is never preshrunk; the cloth will fray easily; and the cloth shrinks from a heavy concentration of cross-stitching and when the finished item has been washed with soap and water. None of these characteristics are bad, they are just peculiarities worth knowing.

As for the fraying, treat it in the following manner. Turn under 1/4″ on the raw edges of either the cotton or linen. Press this measurement towards the wrong side of the cloth. Then finish off the raw edges by either: Whipping around the margins with a knotted double strand of thread (Illus. 2); machine-stitching twice 1/8″ from the edges (Illus. 3); or machine zigzag-stitching twice around the piece (Illus. 4).

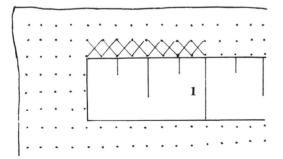

Illus. 1. Aida 8.

Illus. 2. Whipping around the margins.

Illus. 3. Machine-stitching.

Illus. 4. Machine zigzag-stitching.

Threads and Needles

In each cross-stitch key, two brands of six-ply cotton embroidery floss are given. The J. & P. Coats six-strand floss is listed first because that is what I use. Many embroiderers are die-hard DMC fans (their six-strand cotton is also referred to as mouliné spécial), so I have included that preference, too. The final choice in the battle of the brands is up to you. Both products are excellent. However, on the DMC colors, I usually watch the reds, oranges, dark blues, and blacks for colorfastness.

Embroidery floss is marketed in skeins of approximately nine yards each. You can use all six strands of the thread or separate it into one, two, or three strands cut into 14″ lengths. Since my artwork uses cotton and linen fabrics in a variety of counts, refer to the chart entitled "Using Six-strand Cotton Embroidery Floss." This tells you the number of strands to use when you cross- or backstitch on different fabrics.

Tapestry needles have blunt points and vary in size from #13 (the largest) to #26 (the smallest). For all the embroidery in this collection, use a #24 needle. Crewel needles are not suitable instruments since they are intended for stitching techniques that pierce and split a fabric.

Using Six-strand Cotton Embroidery Floss

Fabric	Strands of floss needed to cross-stitch	Strands of floss needed to backstitch	Size of tapestry needle
Aida 8 (100% cotton)	3	2	24
Aida 11 (100% cotton)	2	2	24
Maxi-weave Ribband, 14-count (90% polyester and 10% cotton)	3	2	24
Cork linen, pure linen 19-thread count	3	2	24
Skandia Bands, pure linen 20-thread count	2	2	24

Miscellaneous Supplies

Cross-stitching is really an uncomplicated craft. The basic ingredients are usually a fabric, some floss, a needle, and scissors. A few other supplies are useful, and they are:

Thimble.

Threads. Use cotton-covered (wrapped) polyester for machine straight-stitching and general hand-sewing.

Rulers. A 12-inch C-thru is especially helpful.

Graph Paper. This is needed to work out the changing names and dates in certain designs. It is sold in needlecraft shops and office, drafting, and architectural supply stores. I prefer an erasable paper with a grid of 8 (squares) × 8 (squares) to one inch.

Embroidery Hoops. Hoops are not necessary. The cotton and linen fabrics have enough weight to make the stitching easy. If you must, use adjustable tambour frames made of wood or plastic.

Tracing Paper. This translucent paper comes in pads (9″ × 12″, 11″ × 14″, and 18″ × 24″) or in rolls (10 yards × 36″ wide and 50 yards × 36″ wide). It can be purchased in either a white or yellowish color. The light and medium weights are fine for making any of the patterns necessary to finish your cross-stitch projects.

100% Polyester Batting. Poly-fil traditional needle-punched batting is available in seamless sheets of various sizes (45″ × 60″, 72″ × 90″, 81″ × 96″, and 90″ × 108″). It is washable, cuts like fabric, and adds some body and weight to a surface.

Dressmaker's Tracing Paper (Washable and Dry Cleanable). Dressmaker's tracing paper is used to transfer pattern markings to either the right or wrong side of the fabric. Although each packet contains an assortment of coated colored papers, use the white sheets whenever possible. The white markings disappear easily from either the heat of an iron or from washing with warm water and soap. For light- and medium-colored fabrics, select the lightest possible color of dressmaker's tracing paper.

To mark a fabric always place the waxy side of the paper next to the cloth that is to be inscribed. Work on a hard surface and trace over the markings in the pattern with a sewing gadget called a tracing wheel (Illus. 5). Use just enough pressure so that the marks can be seen.

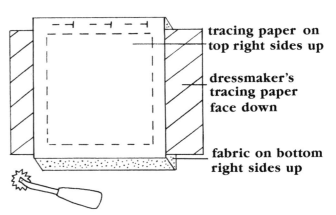

tracing paper on top right sides up

dressmaker's tracing paper face down

fabric on bottom right sides up

Illus. 5. Transferring pattern markings.

Stitching

All the designs in this book are made with either cross-stitches alone or cross-stitches in combination with backstitches. Both stitches are simple to make, and even if you are a complete cross-stitch novice, I encourage you to take the first step. For cross-stitching is relaxing, versatile, and very portable and best of all, it allows you to fulfill your artistic desires at your own time and pace.

Cross-Stitching on Cotton and Linen

In mastering any needlecraft you should start off by learning the basic sewing techniques. I will first describe the process, and the accompanying illustrations will show exactly how it is done.

Cross-stitches are worked by passing a blunt tapestry needle through the holes in a gridlike fabric. A completed cross-stitch is made in two movements: a left-to-right bottom stitch which slants like this / and a right-to-left topstitch which slants like this \. The cross-stitches that result can be made singly (Illus. 6) or embroidered in rows

where the under-stitches are made in one direction, and the returns are worked in the opposite manner (Illus. 7). Cross-stitches can also be sewn in horizontal, vertical, and diagonal directions. The

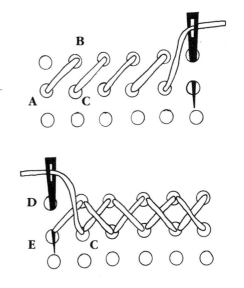

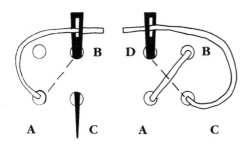

Illus. 6. Single cross-stitch.
a. Bring needle up through hole in fabric at lower left corner of cross (A). Insert thread diagonally across at hole B and come up at C. Pull thread through.
b. Complete other half of cross; stitch from C to D.

Illus. 7. Rows of cross-stitches.
a. Work first strokes left to right. Bring needle up through hole in fabric at A. Insert thread diagonally across at B and come up at C. Pull thread through. Continue to end of row.
b. On return journey, complete other half-cross, sewing right to left. From C go over to D, then under and up to E (same hole as A).

rules state: All the stitches must be crossed in the same direction; you make one cross-stitch within one square on an evenweave cotton fabric (Illus. 8), and; you embroider one cross-stitch over *two* threads of linen (Illus. 9). Like Noah, the patriarch who built the Ark to survive the Flood, start thinking in twos whenever you sew on linen.

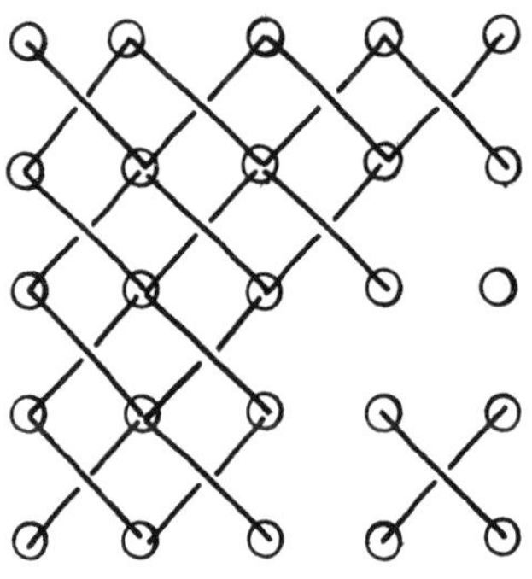

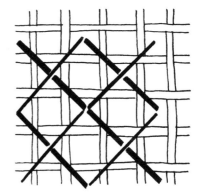

Illus. 8.

Illus. 9

Backstitching on Cotton and Linen

Backstitches (Illus. 10) add detail to a surface which is predominantly marked by X's. Since they are used as accents, they are done after all the cross-stitching is complete. Like cross-stitches they can be sewn in several directions (horizontally, vertically, and diagonally) or in line combinations. On an evenweave cotton fabric, sew one backstitch within one square, but on linen remember to embroider over the two required threads (Illus. 11). On my graphs, backstitches are indicated by a bold line, and they are charted in the direction they are to be sewn.

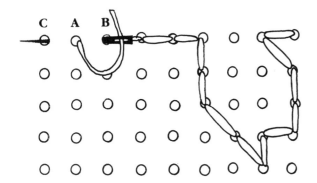

Illus. 10. Backstitch.

1. All stitches are same size.
2. Work right to left even though stitches travel in all directions.
3. Bring needle up through hole in fabric at A.
4. Take small running stitch backwards to B and bring needle up in front of first stitch at C. Pull thread through.
5. Repeat taking another stitch backwards; put needle in same hole as A.

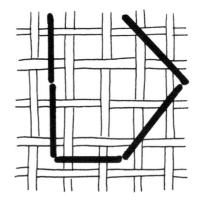

Illus. 11.

The Starting Procedure

Understanding the Charts

Cross-stitch designs are not printed on fabrics. You recreate the embroidery by counting from a graph or chart. As you would expect, the graphs vary in their complexity and the degree of work they require. Mine are divided into four categories: simple, intermediate, advanced, and expert (the most complicated).

As you look at each chart and work on an evenweave cotton, one square on paper represents one square on the fabric that could be filled with a single cross-stitch. For work on linen, one square on paper also equals one cross-stitch, but the cross-stitch is embroidered over *two* threads of linen. The different symbols in the design represent where a cross-stitch should be made and which color needs to be used. Plain squares are undecorated areas of cloth.

The First Cross-Stitch

In the project section of the book, you will repeatedly see the heading "Making the first cross-stitch." Very specific instructions follow this phrase. For example, "Measure across 3 1/4″ from top left corner; measure downwards 4″ from top left corner. Mark point where two measurements intersect (Illus. 12). Start sewing at arrow." If you follow these directions, you will usually make your first cross-stitch at a temporarily marked spot on the fabric, which corresponds to an arrow, which is almost always in the top left corner of the graph (Illus. 13). Refer to the cross-stitch key, and select the specific color of floss. Then continue by making all the cross-stitches to the right. Sew the rest of the design by moving from left to right and from top to bottom.

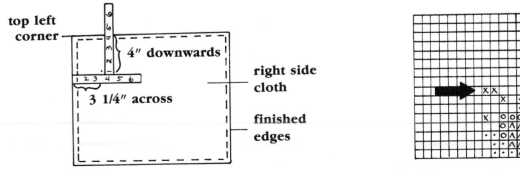

Illus. 12. Intersection point.

Illus. 13. Top left corner of graph.

Starting a Thread

After you have cut and separated your floss into the proper number of strands, do not knot the end. Leave, instead, a one-inch tail of floss hanging against the back of the cloth. Make your first cross-stitches as, at the the same time, you anchor the tail with the next few stitches (Illus. 14).

To begin a new thread after you have already worked several rows of embroidery, run your needle under four or five previously worked stitches on the reverse side of the cloth (Illus. 15). Come up on the right side of the fabric, and cross-stitch as usual.

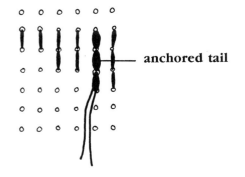

anchored tail

Illus. 14.

Illus. 15.

Carrying Threads

You do not have to finish off your embroidery floss when one color ends, if it reappears again, and if the thread can be run under previous stitches. If, for example, you are making a red flower petal and the color reintroduces itself one-inch away in a second petal, do not end the color in the first position. Instead, carry the floss to an out-of-the-way place, come up on the right side of the cloth, take one running stitch, and then let the thread dangle until it is needed again (Illus. 16). At that point, rethread it, duck under the previous stitches on the wrong side of the cloth, and travel to the new location. Continue sewing as usual. The one exception to this principle involves wide-open spaces. Try not to carry a thread across an opening of 5/8″ or more. Loose unsupported threads tend to look ugly when they show through the front of an article.

red

red

Illus. 16.

Ending a Thread

To end a thread run your needle under four or five stitches on the back of the design and clip off the excess floss. Remember that the reverse side of the fabric should be as neat in appearance as the front. Therefore, no hanging threads.

Washing and Ironing Techniques

Once the needlework is done, it needs to be hand- or machine-washed before you proceed to the "finishing directions." Even if the embroidery appears clean, launder it anyway. In the case of the samplers and the wooden products, this may be the last time the piece is ever cleaned. Washing also shrinks the fabric and gives the stitching a nice neat over-all look. For hand-washing use lukewarm water and a gentle soap. Wash and rinse it a number of times. Then roll the wet article in a turkish towel to remove the excess moisture. Hang the cloth so it is flat and wrinkle-free. For machine-washing, set the controls on warm water and a gentle cycle. After that place the cloth in the dryer, but remove it while the fabric is still damp.

With the iron set on cotton and steam, press the embroidery on both sides. Then lay the article flat until it is thoroughly dried.

Cross-Stitch Recap

Many of the cross-stitch procedures are repetitive. Instead of providing this basic information for each project, I am listing it once. I assume, therefore, that when you look at the "Finishing directions," you have already completed this basic routine, unless stated otherwise.

1. Do not preshrink evenweave cottons or linens. Do, however, preshrink any of the cottons which will be used as linings, backings, or supporting fabrics. Preshrink also any laces, ribbons, or ruffles.

2. Cut your evenweave fabric to the exact measurements given. On most projects (the place mats and bookmarks are the few exceptions) I have included 3″ seam allowances within these dimensions. Evenweave fabrics fray. Finish off the raw edges by either hand- or machine-stitching (see Illus. 2–4).

3. In the upper left corner of the fabric, find the starting point for the first cross-stitch (see Illus. 12). On the charted design this same reference point will be marked by an arrow (see Illus. 13), which means start sewing here.

4. Do the embroidery by referring to the graph and cross-stitch key. See the chart for the correct number of strands of floss to be used for cross- and backstitching on your particular fabric. For work on cotton remember that one square on paper represents one square on a fabric that can be filled with a single cross-stitch. For work on linen, one square on paper also equals one cross-stitch, but the cross-stitch is embroidered over *two* threads of linen. Backstitches are indicated by a bold line, and they are charted in the direction they are to be sewn. Sew all the cross-stitches first; add the backstitches later.

5. Wash the finished embroidery. Press. Let it completely dry.

6. Consult the "Finishing directions" provided for each project.

7. Make all patterns that are required with tracing paper, pencil, and ruler.

8. To transfer any pattern markings to the right or wrong side of a fabric, always use the lightest possible color of dressmaker's tracing paper and a tracing wheel. White and yellow are preferable, but white is far better if the color can be seen. To use this paper see Illus. 5.

9. In the project diagrams which accompany the "Finishing directions," an (R) means that the fabric is right side up; a (W) means that the fabric is wrong side up.

Mounting and Framing

Materials and Techniques

White matboard
Poly-fil traditional batting (100% polyester)
Bleached muslin
One-inch masking tape
White six-strand cotton floss
Regular sewing thread
Ruler
Mat knife
Pliers
Large crewel needle
Straight pins

In the instructions of the projects that require mounting and framing, there is a heading "Margin to be added at mounting." It is here that you are asked to add a specified margin (3/4″ to 1 1/2″) to all four sides of a particular design before the mounting procedure can begin. These additional inches, which butt into the usual 3-inch seam allowances, give a breather between the edge of the embroidery and the edge of the frame. To mount, for example, a sampler like "Our Love Should Not Be Just Words and Talk" (1″ borders required), follow this basic routine:

1. On one side of the artwork, locate the very edge of the design. Measure 1″ (this number changes) beyond this point; mark the spot with a straight pin. On the three remaining sides of the picture, mark the 1″ borders. Measure from the edge of the design. Pin.

2. With a knotted single strand of thread, connect these four points. To do so, hand-stitch these lines by following one row in the fabric and by weaving in and out of the cloth with 1″ running stitches. These stitched lines are now the edges of your needlework.

3. Measure the length and width of this newly stitched shape (Illus. 17).

4. Cut three pieces of matboard, each measuring the dimensions in Step 3. Stack them together; tape in a north-south-east-west position (Illus. 18).

5. Cut one piece of polyester batting measuring the dimensions in Step 3. Lay the batting over the boards.

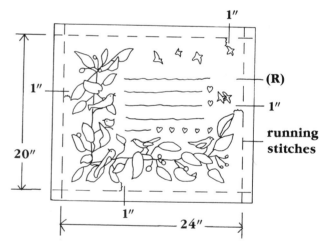

Illus. 17. Measuring the length and width.

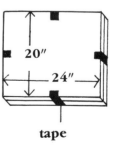

Illus. 18. Three matboards.

6. Cut one piece of muslin; add a 2-inch seam allowance to all sides of the dimensions in Step 3. With right sides up, center the muslin over the batting/matboard combination. On the back, fold in the top and bottom. Tape. Fold in the sides. Tape temporarily (Illus. 19).

7. With right sides down, lay the embroidery flat; lay the muslin/batting/matboard combination on top and within the stitched edges of the design.

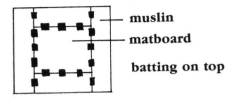

Illus. 19. View of back.

Fold in the top and bottom. Tape. Fold in the sides. Tape. Get the corners neat and flat.

8. On the back of the design, sew the four corners flat with 1/2″ running stitches. Use a crewel needle and six-strand cotton floss. If necessary, use pliers to pull the needle through.

9. While still on the back, lace back and forth between the finished-off edges of the top and bottom. To do, start at one side and work towards the other. Cut the floss into two-yard lengths. Insert the needle 3/16″ beyond the folded and stitched edges of the cloth (Illus. 20). As you approach the end of each thread, check to see that the edge of the design line rests on the edge of the matboard.

Check also to see that the needlework is centered, flat, and slightly taut.

10. Lace in the opposite direction and in the same manner (Illus. 21).

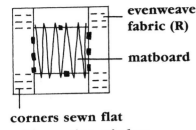

Illus. 20. View of back.

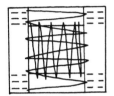

Illus. 21. View of back.

11. Remove the edge of the design threads and any tape.

12. Add a frame. Glass or Plexiglas is not necessary.

PROJECTS

Heart and House

Home Sweet Home (Place Mat)

Quote: Opera Clari, the Maid of Milan. *John Howard Payne*
Degree of work: simple
Fabric: aida 11, ivory
Cut size of cloth needed: 20" wide × 14"
Finished size: place mat approximately 18" wide × 12", 18 1/2" square napkin

Cross-Stitch Key

Symbol	J. & P. Coats six-strand floss Color	or DMC six-strand
·	75-A Tropic Orange	920
⊠	81-B Dk. Colonial Brown	801
⊙	61 Ecru	822
■	Use DMC color	642
◆	12 Black	310
Ⓢ	215 Apple Green	471
③	109 Dk. Willow Green	367
=	24-A Oriental Blue	518
△	226 Pearl Pink	963
□	Cloth as is	

Backstitch Key

Symbol	J. & P. Coats six-strand floss Color	or DMC six-strand
⊞	12 Black	310

Area of Backstitch: *12 Black—All.*

Purchase one skein of each color.

In color page G.

Making the first cross-stitch: Measure across 2 1/4" from top left corner; measure downwards 3/4" from top left corner. Mark point where two measurements intersect. Start sewing at arrow.

Other materials: Brown floral print, for back and napkin—5/8 yard. Poly-fil traditional batting, 100% polyester—20" wide × 14".

Finishing directions

1. Make place mat (Illus. 22) and napkin (Illus. 23) patterns.

2. With right sides up, place pattern over embroidery. Get stitching lines at top of pattern to rest

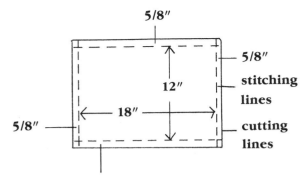

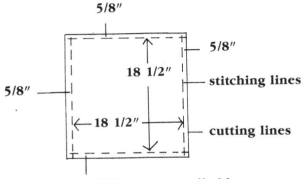

add 5/8″ seams to all sides

Illus. 22. Place mat front: Cut one of embroidered aida. Back: Cut one of brown print. Batting: Cut one.

add 5/8″ seams to all sides

Illus. 23. Napkin: Cut one of brown print.

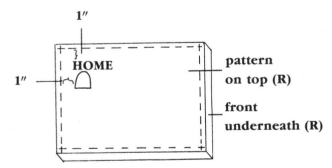

Illus. 24.

1″ above word "HOME"; get stitching lines on left side of pattern to rest 1″ from left side of shield (Illus. 24). Pin pattern to cloth. Cut. Transfer stitching lines to wrong side of front.

3. Lay out and cut batting, back, and napkin. Before patterns are unpinned from batting and napkin, transfer stitching lines to wrong side.

4. Place back wrong side up. Position batting on top, stitching lines showing. Pin together.

5. With right sides together and seams matching, place front over back/batting. Pin. Machine straight-stitch, pivoting at corners. Leave 4″ opening in middle of bottom (Illus. 25).

6. Trim seams to 1/2″. Turn. Press fabric at opening inwards.

7. Machine topstitch 1/8″ from edges of mat (Illus. 26).

8. Make napkin. Place napkin right side down. Press 5/8″ seams inward along stitching lines. Turn under 1/4″ on raw edge. Press and pin. Corners should look alike. Stitch close to inner folded edge (Illus. 27).

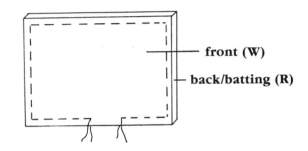

Illus. 25.

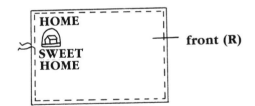

Illus. 26.

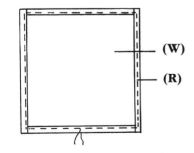

Illus. 27.

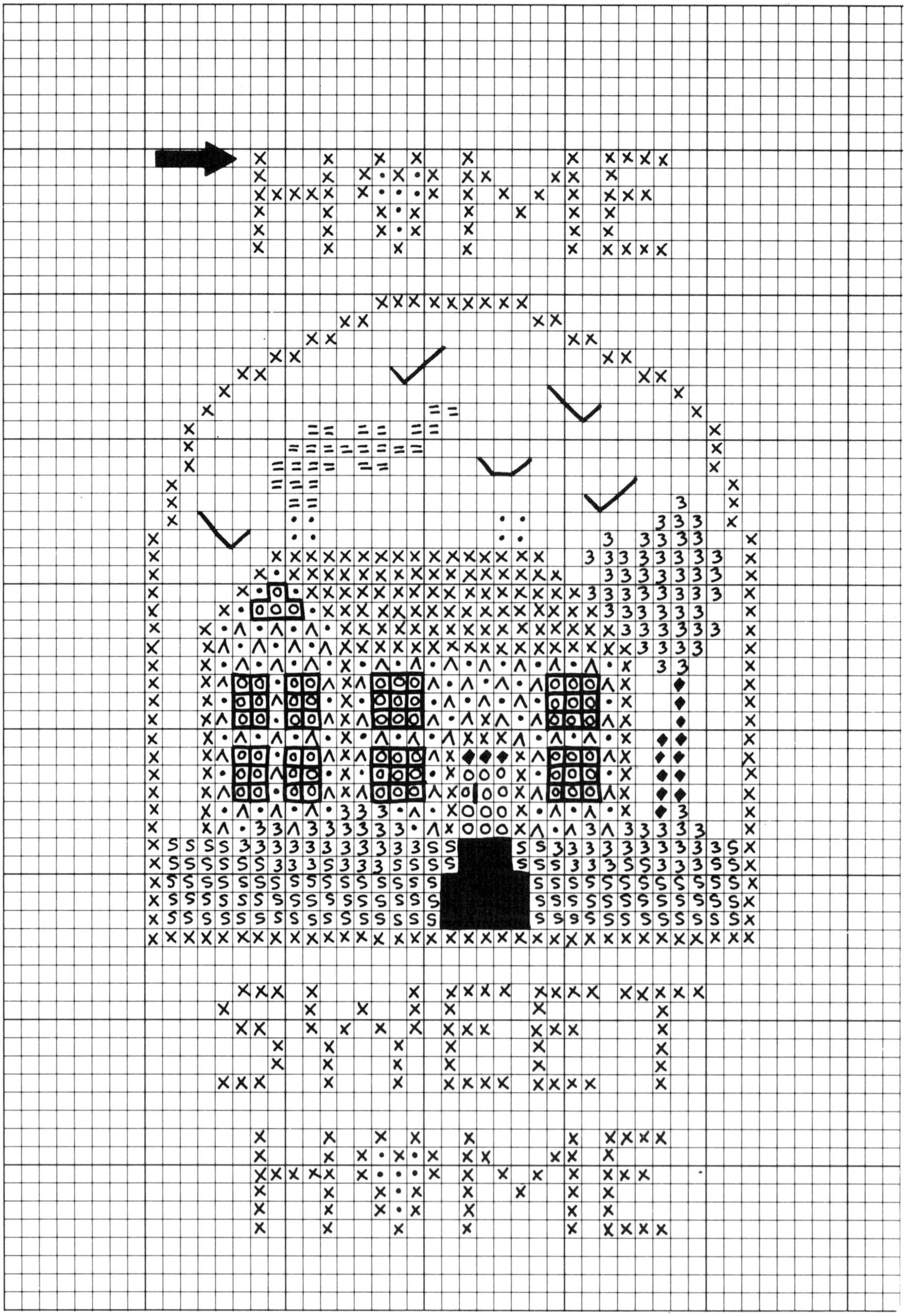

Illus. 28. Charted graph.

Bless Our Home (Place Mat)

Quote: unknown
Degree of work: simple
Fabric: aida 11, white
Cut size of cloth needed: 22" wide × 17"
Finished size: place mat approximately 18" wide × 12 3/4", 18 1/2" square napkin

Cross-Stitch Key

Symbol	J. & P. Coats six-strand floss Color	or DMC six-strand
⊠	28 Myrtle	700
•	245 Atlantic Blue	799
=	75-A Tropic Orange	920
S	231 Goldenrod	742
O	12 Black	310
■	1 White	Snow-White
◩	Use DMC color	355
□	Cloth as is	

Backstitch Key

Symbol	J. & P. Coats six-strand floss Color	or DMC six-strand
⊞	28 Myrtle	700

Area of Backstitch: *28 Myrtle—Flower stems.*

Purchase two skeins of 28 Myrtle. Buy one skein of each remaining color.

Making the first cross-stitch: Measure across 3" from top corner side; measure downwards 2 1/2" from top left corner. Mark point where two measurements intersect. Start sewing at arrow.

Other materials: Green dotted cotton, for back and napkin—5/8 yard. Poly-fil traditional batting, 100% polyester—20" wide × 15".

Finishing directions

1. Make place mat pattern (Illus. 29). Use Illus. 23 for napkin.

In color page G.

2. With right sides up, place pattern over embroidery. Get pattern so there is 1/2" space between topstitching line and top green border, and there is 7/8" space on either side between side stitching lines and ends of green borders (Illus. 30). Pin pattern to cloth. Cut. Transfer stitching lines to wrong side front.

3. Repeat Steps 3–8 in "Home Sweet Home."

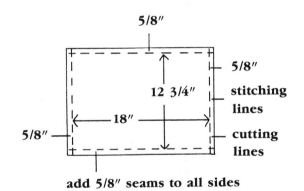

Illus. 29. Place mat front: Cut one embroidered aida. Back: Cut one of green dotted fabric. Batting: Cut one.

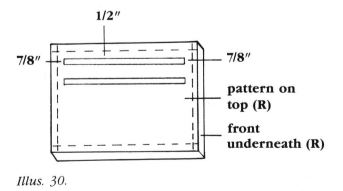

Illus. 30.

23

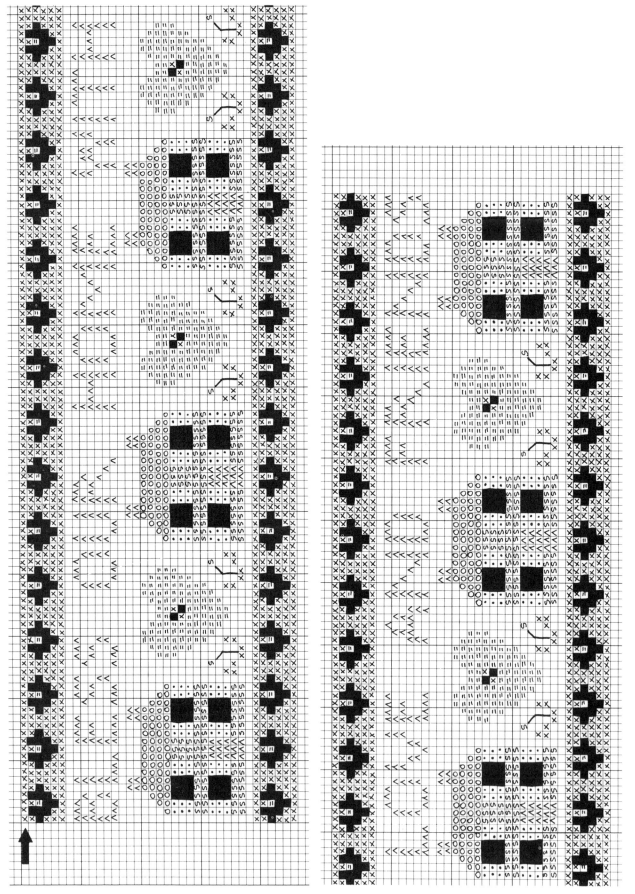

Illus. 31. Charted graph.

East, West, Home Is Best (Wall Hanging)

Quote: John Ploughman. *Charles Haddon Spurgeon*
Degree of work: intermediate
Fabric: aida 11, white
Cut size of cloth needed: 10" wide × 22"
Finished size: approximately 6" wide × 16 1/4"

Cross-Stitch Key

Symbol	Color (J. & P. Coats six-strand floss)	or DMC six-strand
O	245 Atlantic Blue	799
=	55 Navy	823
△	69 Lt. Steel Blue	809
⊠	76 China Blue	825
•	8 Blue	800
e	62 Russet	435
⁄	213 Beige	644
□	Cloth as is	

Backstitch Key

Symbol	Color (J. & P. Coats six-strand floss)	or DMC six-strand
⊞	62 Russet	435
	76 China Blue	825

Area of Backstitch: *62 Russet*—the pole on the smallest boat. *76 China Blue*—all other details in the verse and the decorative square.

Purchase two skeins of 76 China Blue. Buy one skein of each remaining color.

Making the first cross-stitch: Measure across 2 3/4" from top left corner; measure downwards 4 3/4" from top left corner. Mark point where two measurements intersect. Start sewing at arrow.

Other materials: Blue and white gingham, for back—10" wide × 22". Wooden rod hangers with chain—7 3/8" long including knobs.

Finishing directions

1. Add borders to design. Add 3/8" to sides (measure from outside blue square). Add 2 3/4" to top (measure from top of "East") and bottom

In color page E.

(measure from bottom blue square). Mark with pins. Using knotted single strand of white thread, hand-stitch these lines by following one row in aida and by weaving in and out cloth with 1" running stitches (Illus. 32).

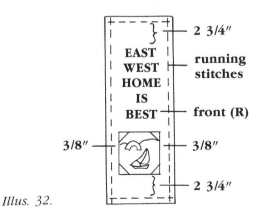

Illus. 32.

2. With right sides together, place front over back. Pin. Machine-stitch, pivoting at corners. Sew right on running stitches, leaving 3" opening in middle of top (Illus. 33).

25

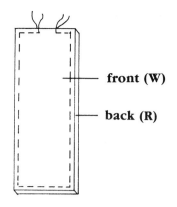

Illus. 33.

front (W)

back (R)

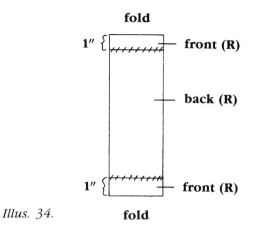

Illus. 34.

fold

1" { front (R)

back (R)

1" { front (R)

fold

3. Trim seams to 1/4". Turn. Press fabric at opening inwards. Slipstitch opening.

4. Finish off ends. At top and bottom fold 1" of fabric towards back; press. Slipstitch front to back (Illus. 34).

5. Add dowels to top and bottom. Remove knobs, slide wood through 1" sleeves, then replace knobs. Top dowel has chain for hanging.

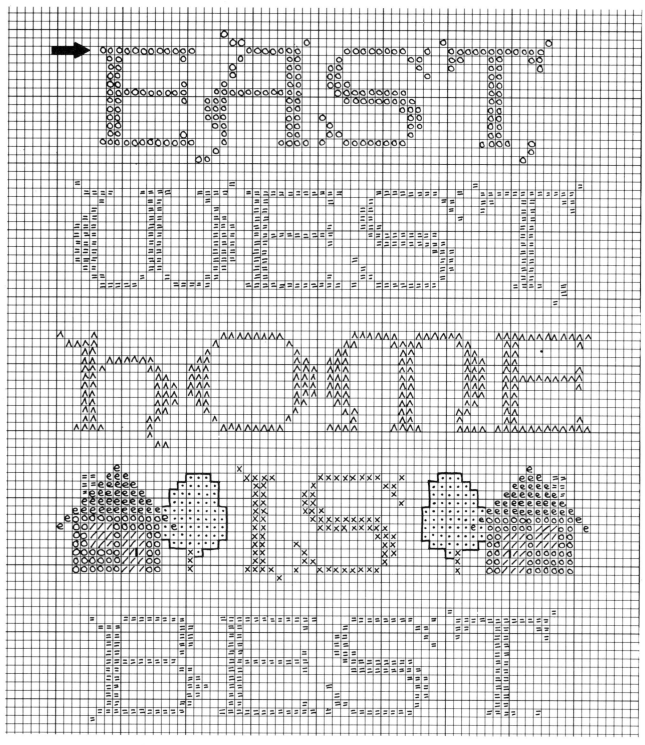

Illus. 35. Charted graph.

Illus. 35. (cont).

Be It Ever So Humble (Pillow)

Quote: Opera *Clari, The Maid of Milan.* John Howard Payne
Degree of work: intermediate
Fabric: aida 11, ivory
Cut size of cloth needed: 17 1/2" square
Finished size: approximately 13" square

Cross-Stitch Key

Symbol	J. & P. Coats six-strand floss Color	or DMC six-strand
⧄	*55 Navy*	*823*
③	*69 Lt. Steel Blue*	*809*
■	*140 Signal Red*	*321*
⊙	*90-A Bright Gold*	*783*
◆	*75-A Tropic Orange*	*920*
◹	*81-B Dk. Colonial Brown*	*801*
Ⓜ	*1 White*	*Snow-White*
ⓢ	*71 Pewter Grey*	*415*
⊟	*28 Myrtle*	*700*
ⓔ	*98 Fern Green*	*989*
Ⓣ	*99 Grass Green*	*703*
·	*109 Dk. Willow Green*	*367*
Ⓤ	*143 Lt. Cardinal*	*815*
⊠	*62 Russet*	*435*
Ⓛ	*12 Black*	*310*
☐	*Cloth as is*	

Backstitch Key

Symbol	J. & P. Coats six-strand floss Color	or DMC six-strand
⊞	*12 Black*	*310*
	81-B Dk. Colonial Brown	*801*
	140 Signal Red	*321*
	99 Grass Green	*703*
	69 Lt. Steel Blue	*809*
	55 Navy	*823*

Area of backstitch—Within house rectangle: *12 Black*—Railing on top of house; fencing; lines within shutters; doorknob; and sidewalk lines. *81-B Dk. Colonial Brown*—Edge of roof and dog's tail. *140 Signal Red*—Dog's collar. *99 Grass Green*—Stems on flowers. Flower

In color page B.

repeats: *69 Lt. Steel Blue*—Outline on all leaves and buds. *55 Navy*—All veins and segments within leaves and buds.

Purchase two skeins each of 55 Navy, 69 Lt. Steel Blue, and 90-A Bright Gold. Buy one skein of each remaining color.

Making the first cross-stitch: Measure across 3" from top left corner; measure downwards 3" from top left corner. Mark point where two measurements intersect. Start sewing at arrow.

Other materials: Medium blue cotton for back—3/8 yard. Navy maxi piping—2 1/2 yards. 12" square pillow insert.

Finishing directions

1. Make pillow patterns for front (Illus. 36) and back (Illus. 37).

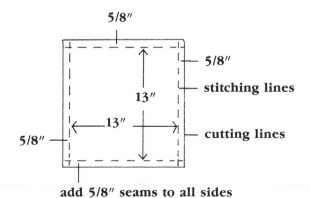

add 5/8" seams to all sides

Illus. 36. Pillow front: Cut one of embroidered aida.

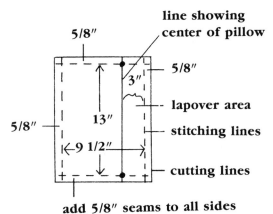

line showing
center of pillow

5/8″

5/8″

3″

13″

9 1/2″

5/8″

lapover area

stitching lines

cutting lines

add 5/8″ seams to all sides

Illus. 37. Pillow back: Cut two of blue cotton.

2. With right sides up, lay front pattern over embroidery. Center design (borders should be about 7/8″ on all sides). Pin. Cut cloth. Transfer stitching lines to wrong side front.

3. Lay out and cut back. Transfer stitching lines and dots to wrong side.

4. Baste piping to right side front. Begin in middle of one side. Position folded edge of piping towards center of design. Turn end downwards at start, and arrange so stitching on piping rests on stitching line transferred to wrong side front. Overlap ends by 1 1/2″; turn end downward (Illus. 38).

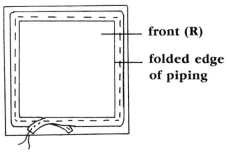

front (R)

folded edge of piping

Illus. 38.

5. On back sections turn in center edge along seam line. Press. Turn under 1/4″ on raw edge. Press. Pin. Machine-stitch close to inner edge (Illus. 39).

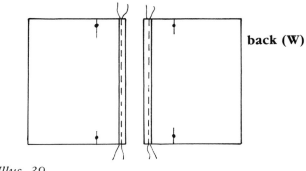

back (W)

Illus. 39.

6. With right sides down, pin left back on right back matching large ●'s. Machine-stitch across lapover area (Illus. 40).

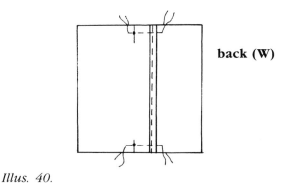

back (W)

Illus. 40.

7. With right sides together pin back on front with piping wedged between. Machine-stitch, pivoting at corners. Trim seams to 1/2″ (Illus. 41).

8. Turn. Push insert through slit in back.

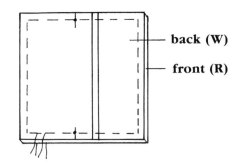

back (W)

front (R)

Illus. 41.

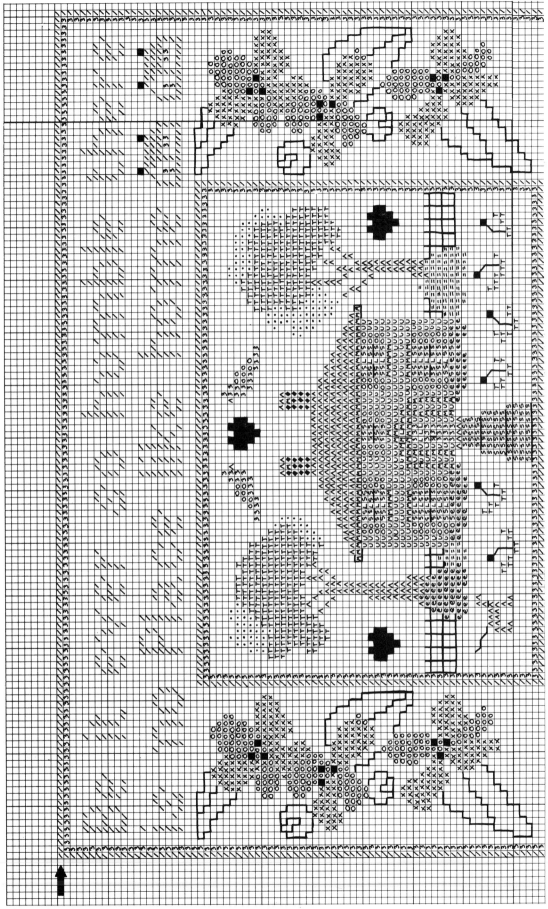

Illus. 42. Charted graph.

Illus. 42. (cont.).

Instructions for this sampler begin on p. 117.

"Wedding Sampler," p. 98.

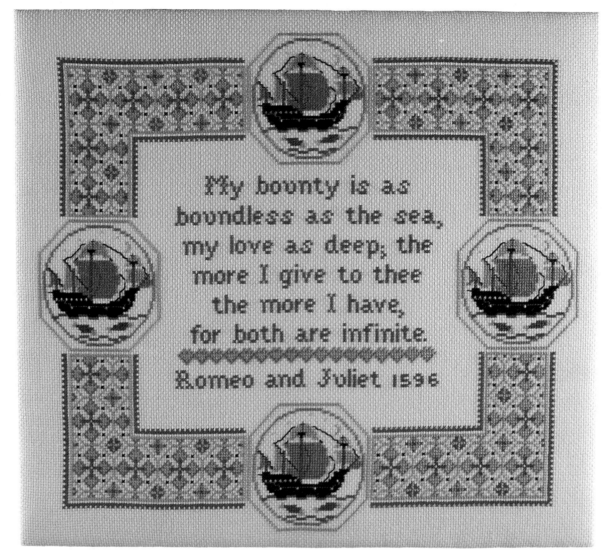

"Romeo and Juliet," p. 108.

Pillow, p. 29.

Tote bag, p. 71; handbag, p. 68; bread cloth, p. 62.

B

Above: Serving tray, p. 85.
Right: "Love Never Ends," p. 104.
Below: "Home Is Where the Heart Is," p. 36.

Photo album cover, p. 65.

Left to right: Belt, p. 60; bookmark, p. 51; bookmark, p. 53.

"Teach Me To Love," p. 120.

D

Left: Wall hanging, p. 25.
Above: Left pillow, p. 43; right pillow, p. 39.
Below: "Love Conquers All," p. 114.

*Yellow guest towel, p. 54; Blue bridal hand
towel, p. 78.*

*Runner, p. 47; left potholder, p. 56;
right potholder, p. 58.*

"Love Bears All Things," p. 101.

"Blessings on This House," p. 33.

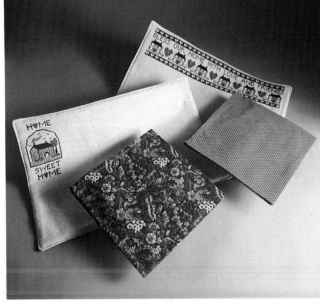

Left place mat, p. 20; right place mat, p. 23.

"Cat Table Runner," p. 74; "Doves," p. 82.

G

Box lid, p. 80; dresser scarf, p. 87.

Bridal pillowcase, p. 92.

"Our Love Should Not Be Just Words and Talk," p. 111.

Blessings on This House (Sampler)

Quote: letter to Abigail Adams from President John Adams
Degree of work: advanced
Fabric: aida 11, ivory
Cut size of cloth needed: 18 1/2" wide × 21 1/2"
Finished size: approximately 14 1/4" wide × 17 1/8"

In color page G.

Cross-Stitch Key

Symbol	J. & P. Coats six-strand floss Color	or DMC six-strand
⊠	75-A Tropic Orange	920
=	81-B Dk. Colonial Brown	801
•	1 White	Snow-White
U	62 Russet	435
3	5-A Chartreuse	704
△	99 Grass Green	703
e	28 Myrtle	700
⟋	90-A Bright Gold	783
O	43 Dk. Yellow	744
◆	258 Golden Toast	977
C	143 Lt. Cardinal	815
■	213 Beige	644
s	81 Dk. Brown	434
☐	Cloth as is	

Backstitch Key

Symbol	J. & P. Coats six-strand floss Color	or DMC six-strand
	99 Grass Green	703
	90-A Bright Gold	783
	62 Russet	435
	143 Lt. Cardinal	815
	81-B Dk. Colonial Brown	801

Area of backstitch: *99 Grass Green*—Stems in border. *90-A Bright Gold*—Sides on house. *62 Russet*—Windowpanes, stair steps, and all details in center of house except on door. *143 Lt. Cardinal*—Windowpanes on door. *81-B Dk. Colonial Brown*—Doorknob.

Purchase three skeins of 99 Grass Green and two skeins each of 75-A Tropic Orange and 43 Dk. Yellow. Buy one skein of each remaining color.

Making the first cross-stitch: Measure across 3" from top left corner; measure downwards 3" from top left corner. Mark point where two measurements intersect. Start sewing at arrow.

Areas of special concern: Initials and date change. See letters #2 and numbers #2. There are 83 spaces available between green circles at bottom. Leave one space between initials and periods. Leave one space between each number within date. Leave 5 spaces between initials and date (ignore last period). Center line. Work details out on graph paper.

Finishing directions: See "Mounting and Framing."

Margin to be added at mounting: Add 1 1/8" borders.

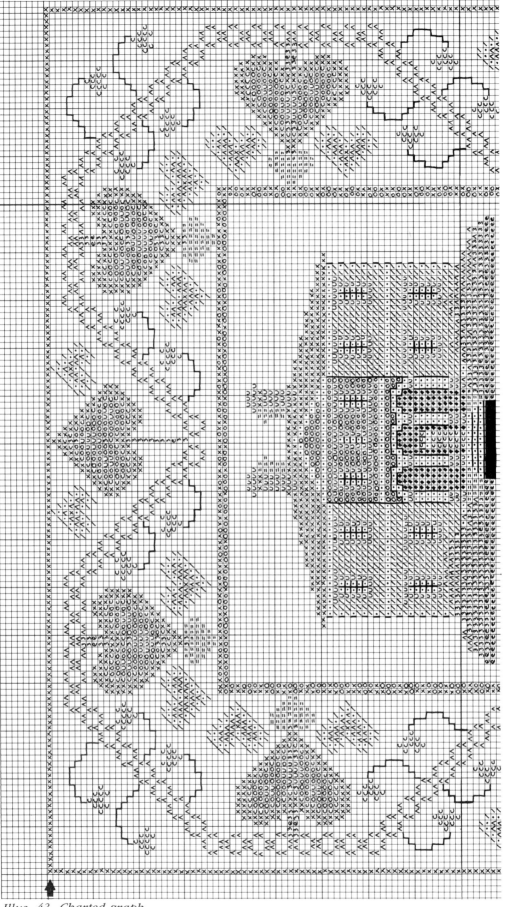

Illus. 43. Charted graph.

Illus. 43. (cont.).

Home Is Where the Heart Is (Sampler)

Quote: attributed to Pliny
Degree of work: advanced
Fabric: aida 11, ivory
Cut size of cloth needed: 18 1/2" wide × 16"
Finished size: approximately 14 1/4" wide ×
11 3/4"

Cross-Stitch Key

Symbol	J. & P. Coats six-strand floss Color	or DMC six-strand
=	*Use DMC color*	*414*
3	*1 White*	*Snow-White*
△	*71 Pewter Grey*	*415*
■	*12 Black*	*310*
U	*8 Blue*	*800*
•	*70 Silver Grey*	*762*
◆	*75-A Tropic Orange*	*920*
O	*81 Dk. Brown*	*434*
M	*90-A Bright Gold*	*783*
⊠	*69 Lt. Steel Blue*	*809*
T	*5-A Chartreuse*	*704*
◺	*99 Grass Green*	*703*
Z	*28 Myrtle*	*700*
▣	*Use DMC color*	*369*
◿	*26 Nile Green*	*966*
S	*143 Lt. Cardinal*	*815*
☐	*Cloth as is*	

In color page C.

Backstitch Key

Symbol	J. & P. Coats six-strand floss Color	or DMC six-strand
⊞	*Use DMC color*	*414*
	12 Black	*310*

Area of Backstitch: *DMC 414*—Roof edges on right and left; corners of porch roof; and long single line above front porch. *12 Black*—All other details on house, sidewalk, and light.

Purchase two skeins of 69 Lt. Steel Blue. Buy one skein of each remaining color.

Making the first cross-stitch: Measure across 3 1/2" from top left corner; measure downwards 3" from top left corner. Mark point where two measurements intersect. Start sewing at arrow.

Finishing directions: See "Mounting and Framing."

Margin to be added at mounting: Add 1" borders

Illus. 44. Charted graph.

Illus. 44. (cont.).

Love Makes a House a Home (Pillow)

Quote: paraphrase from Home. *Edgar A. Guest*
Degree of work: advanced
Fabric: cork linen, 19-thread count, cream
Cut size of cloth needed: 22" wide × 18"
Finished size: 17" wide × 13 1/4"

In color page E.

Cross-Stitch Key

Symbol	J. & P. Coats six-strand floss	or DMC six-strand
	Color	
⊠	140 Signal Red	321
•	Use DMC color	414
■	1 White	Snow-White
L	8 Blue	800
◺	245 Atlantic Blue	799
U	71 Pewter Grey	415
◆	12 Black	310
S	28 Myrtle	700
e	5-A Chartreuse	704
=	216 Avocado	469
╱	81 Dk. Brown	434
3	Use DMC color	642
O	91 Emerald Green	913
T	109 Dk. Willow Green	367
M	223 Sun Gold	743
C	75-A Tropic Orange	920
N	65 Beauty Pink	776
◢	98 Fern Green	989
☐	Cloth as is	

Backstitch Key

Symbol	J. & P. Coats six-strand floss	or DMC six-strand
	Color	
⊞	12 Black	310

Area of Backstitch: *12 Black*—All.

Purchase two skeins each of 140 Signal Red, 8 Blue, 81 Dk. Brown, DMC 642, and 91 Emerald Green. Buy one skein of each remaining color.

Making the first cross-stitch: Measure across 3" from top left corner; measure downwards 3 1/4" from top left corner. Mark point where two measurements intersect. Start sewing at arrow.

Other materials: Red cotton, for back—3/8 yard. Red maxi-piping—2 1/2 yards. Beige cotton for pillow insert—1/2 yard. Poly-fil 100% polyester fibre—6 ounces.

Finishing directions

1. Repeat Steps 1–7 in "Be It Ever So Humble." The only exceptions are: At Step 1 make these patterns (Illus. 45 and 46), and at Step 2, borders are about 1".

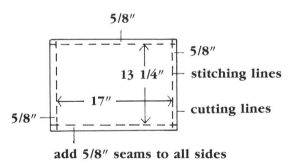

5/8"

5/8"

13 1/4" ← **stitching lines**

17"

5/8" ← **cutting lines**

5/8"

add 5/8" seams to all sides

Illus. 45. Pillow front: Cut one of embroidered linen. Insert: Cut two of beige cotton.

2. Turn pillow. Press.

3. Lay out and cut insert. Before pattern is unpinned transfer stitching lines to wrong side both pieces.

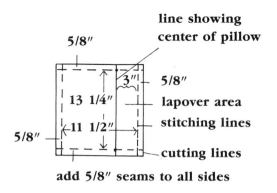

line showing
center of pillow

5/8"

5/8"

13 1/4"

3"

lapover area

stitching lines

11 1/2"

5/8"

cutting lines

add 5/8" seams to all sides

Illus. 46. Pillow back: Cut two of red cotton.

4. With right sides together, machine-stitch insert sections, pivoting at corners. Leave 4" opening in middle of one side.

5. Turn insert. Press fabric at opening inwards.

6. Stuff insert firmly with polyester fibre. Slipstitch opening. Push insert through slit in back.

Illus. 47. Charted graph.

41

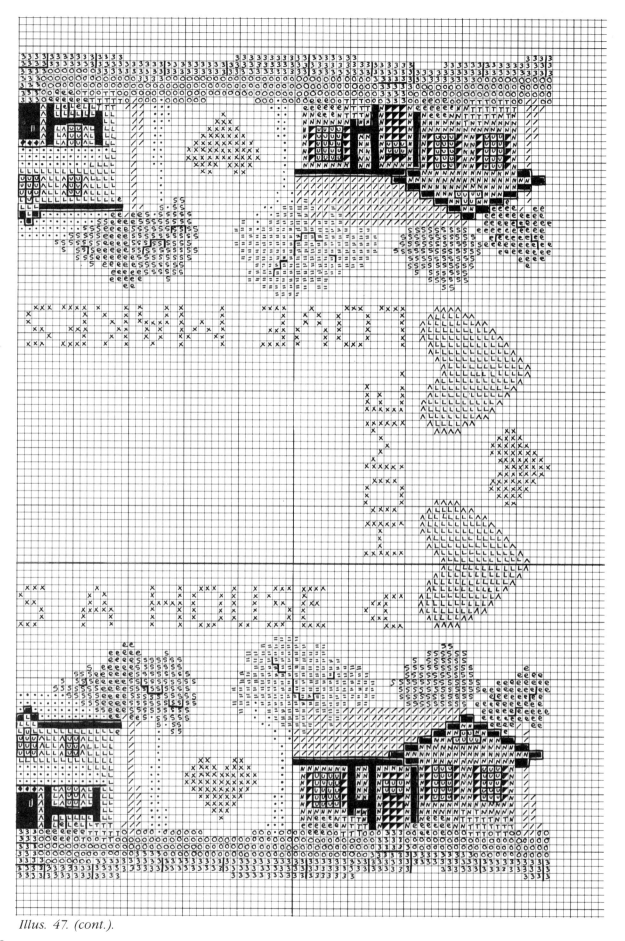

Illus. 47. (cont.).

Where We Love Is Home (Pillow)

Quote: Homesick in Heaven. *Oliver Wendell Holmes*
Degree of work: advanced
Fabric: aida 11, white
Cut size of cloth needed: 21 1/2" wide × 17"
Finished size: approximately 18 1/2" wide x 13 3/4" without ruffle

Cross-Stitch Key

	J. & P. Coats six-strand floss	or DMC six-strand
Symbol	**Color**	
⊠	140 Signal Red	321
·	215 Apple Green	471
3	62 Russet	435
=	1 White	Snow-White
◺	81-B Dk. Colonial Brown	801
○	90-A Bright Gold	783
▽	91 Emerald Green	913
■	239 Imperial Blue	995
S	213 Beige	644
◿	24-A Oriental Blue	518
☐	Cloth as is	

Backstitch Key

	J. & P. Coats six-strand floss	or DMC six-strand
Symbol	**Color**	
⊞	81-B Dk. Colonial Brown	801
	62 Russet	435
	140 Signal Red	321

Area of Backstitch: *81-B Dk. Colonial Brown*—Vertical lines on house; doorknobs on both houses; and birds. *62 Russet*—Lines within window, and outline around dog's head, feet, and tail. *140 Signal Red*—Check lines.

Purchase three skeins each of 140 Signal Red and 90-A Bright Gold. Purchase two skeins each of 215 Apple Green, 62 Russet, and 91 Emerald Green. Buy one skein of each remaining color.

In color page E.

Making the first cross-stitch: Measure across 2 1/2" from top left corner; measure downwards 2 1/8" from top left corner. Mark point where two measurements intersect. Start sewing at arrow.

Other materials: Red and white gingham, for ruffle—1/2 yard. Solid red cotton, for back—1/2 yard. White cotton, for pillow insert—1/2 yard. Poly-fil 100% polyester fiber—14 ounces.

Finishing directions

1. Repeat Steps 1–3 in " Be It Ever So Humble." The only exceptions are: At Step 1 make these patterns (Illus. 48 and 49), and; At Step 2, borders are about 3/4".

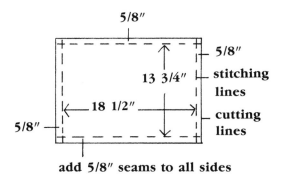

add 5/8" seams to all sides

Illus. 48. Pillow front: Cut one of embroidered aida. Insert: Cut two of white cotton.

2. Cut ruffle. Cut 4 strips of fabric each 4" wide and 44" long.

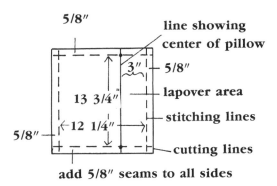

5/8"

line showing
center of pillow

3" — 5/8"

13 3/4" —— lapover area

12 1/4" —— stitching lines

5/8" —

—— cutting lines

add 5/8" seams to all sides

Illus. 49. Pillow back: Cut two of red cotton.

3. With right sides together stitch 4 ruffle sections together; make 1/2" seams. Press seams open (Illus. 50).

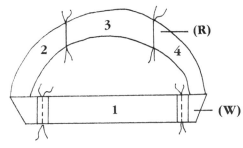

Illus. 50.

4. Narrow-hem lower edge ruffle. To do so, turn up 1/2" seam allowance on lower edge. Press. Turn under 1/4" on raw edge. Press. Pin. Stitch close to inner edge (Illus. 51).

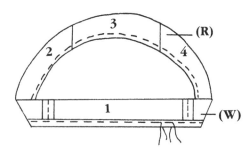

Illus. 51.

5. Gather upper edge ruffle. First, divide ruffle in half; start at one seam and mark midway point at opposite seam. Stitch 1/2" from upper edges using long machine-stitches, breaking at midpoints. Stitch again 1/4" away in seam allowances (Illus. 52).

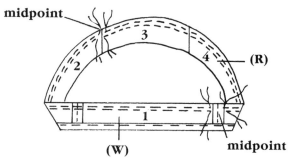

Illus. 52.

6. With right sides together put half ruffle on front. Start by placing one seam in upper left corner and halfway point at lower right corner. Get 1/2" stitching line on ruffle to rest on stitching lines transferred to wrong side front. Evenly adjust gather; pin (Illus. 53).

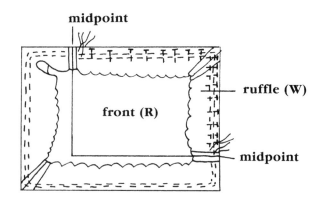

Illus. 53.

7. Gather and pin remaining half ruffle on front.
8. Stitch ruffle to front, pivoting at corners (Illus. 54).

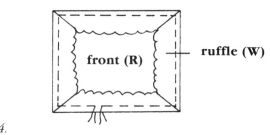

Illus. 54.

9. Repeat Steps 5–7 in "Be It Ever So Humble."
10. Repeat Steps 2–6 in "Love Makes a House a Home."

Illus. 55. Charted graph.

Ilus. 55. (cont.).

Houses, Hearts, and Flowers (Runner)

In color page F.

Degree of work: advanced
Fabric: aida 8, white
Cut size of cloth needed: 18" wide × 42 1/2"
Finished size: approximately 15 1/8" wide × 39"

Cross-Stitch Key

Symbol	J. & P. Coats six-strand floss Color	or DMC six-strand
O	140 Signal Red	321
⊠	143 Lt. Cardinal	815
◣	81 Dk. Brown	434
S	213 Beige	644
e	8 Blue	775
z	109 Dk. Willow Green	367
•	99 Grass Green	703
■	5-A Chartreuse	704
=	46-A Mid Rose	3326
◤	231 Goldenrod	742
L	235 Mint Gold	783
◆	239 Imperial Blue	995
☐	Cloth as is	

Backstitch Key

Symbol	J. & P. Coats six-strand floss Color	or DMC six-strand
⊞	81 Dk. Brown	434
	109 Dk. Willow Green	367

Area of Backstitch: *81 Dk. Brown*—The triangular border; house block—the windows, roof shingles, and tree stem; heart block—the vertical lines; flower block—the handles and horizontal vase lines. *109 Dk. Willow Green*—The flower stems.

Purchase four skeins each of 140 Signal Red, 143 Lt. Cardinal, and 81 Dk. Brown. Purchase two skeins each of 99 Grass Green, 5-A Chartreuse, and 46-A Mid Rose. Buy one skein of each remaining color.

Making the first cross-stitch: Holding cloth vertically, measure 2" from bottom left side; measure 12 1/2" from bottom left edge. Mark point

where two measurements intersect (Illus. 56). Start sewing at arrow, move over to first brown triangle, then sew top of first square with house repeat.

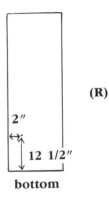

Illus. 56. Intersection of two measurements.

Finishing directions

1. Embroider 12 blocks at bottom of runner. Then turn runner upside down. Along each side sew 62 brown triangles (there are 2 backstitches between each triangle plus one backstitch beyond triangles at either end) (Illus. 57). Sew triangular border at bottom and red surrounding border.
2. From bottom left of runner, count up 17 triangles. At bottom of 17th triangle, sew top of first square with house repeat (Illus. 58). Sew eleven remaining blocks.
3. Wash.
4. On all sides of aida, count 8 squares beyond red border. Mark with pins. Using knotted single strand of thread, hand-stitch these lines by following one row in aida and by weaving in and out cloth with 1" running stitches.

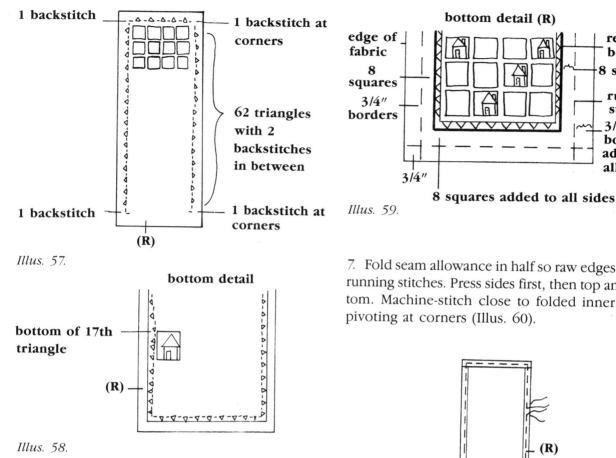

1 backstitch ——— ——— **1 backstitch at corners**

62 triangles with 2 backstitches in between

1 backstitch ——— ——— **1 backstitch at corners**

(R)

Illus. 57.

bottom detail

bottom of 17th triangle ———

(R) ———

Illus. 58.

5. Beyond 8-square border add an additional 3/4″ seam allowance. Cut off excess fabric (Illus. 59).
6. Fold seam allowance towards wrong side on running stitch lines. Press sides first, then top and bottom.

bottom detail (R)

edge of fabric ——— ——— **red border**

8 squares ——— ——— **8 squares**

——— **running stitches**

3/4″ borders ——— **3/4″ borders added to all sides**

3/4″ ———

8 squares added to all sides

Illus. 59.

7. Fold seam allowance in half so raw edges touch running stitches. Press sides first, then top and bottom. Machine-stitch close to folded inner edge, pivoting at corners (Illus. 60).

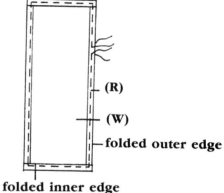

——— **(R)**

——— **(W)**

——— **folded outer edge**

folded inner edge ———

Illus. 60.

Illus. 61. Charted graph.

Illus. 61. (cont.).

Gifts of Love and Friendship

Hearts, Diamonds, and Checks (Bookmark)

Degree of work: simple
Fabric: linen Skandia Band, 20-thread count, ecru with red selvages, 2 1/4" wide
Cut size of cloth needed: 13" long
Finished size: approximately 2 1/4" wide × 9 1/2"

Cross-Stitch Key		
J. & P. Coats six-strand floss		**or DMC six-strand**
Symbol	**Color**	
☐(O)	*12 Black*	*310*
☒	*140 Signal Red*	*321*
☐(e)	*253 Daffodil*	*444*
☐(·)	*Use DMC color*	*208*
☐	*Cloth as is*	

Purchase one skein of each color.

Making the first cross-stitch: Measure 1 1/4" from top folded edge of linen. Start sewing at arrow.

Finishing directions

1. Finish off ends of bookmark. With right sides up, turn top back 1/2"; press. Turn under 1/4" on raw edge; press. Slipstitch folded inner edge. At

In color page D.

opposite end, machine-stitch close to bottom (Illus. 62).

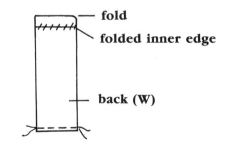

fold
folded inner edge

back (W)

Illus. 62.

2. Do embroidery.
3. Finish off bookmark bottom. Measure 1 1/4" beyond end of embroidery, press back fabric. Add 1/2" seam allowance; cut off excess cloth. Turn under 1/4" on raw edges. Press. Slipstitch folded inner edge.

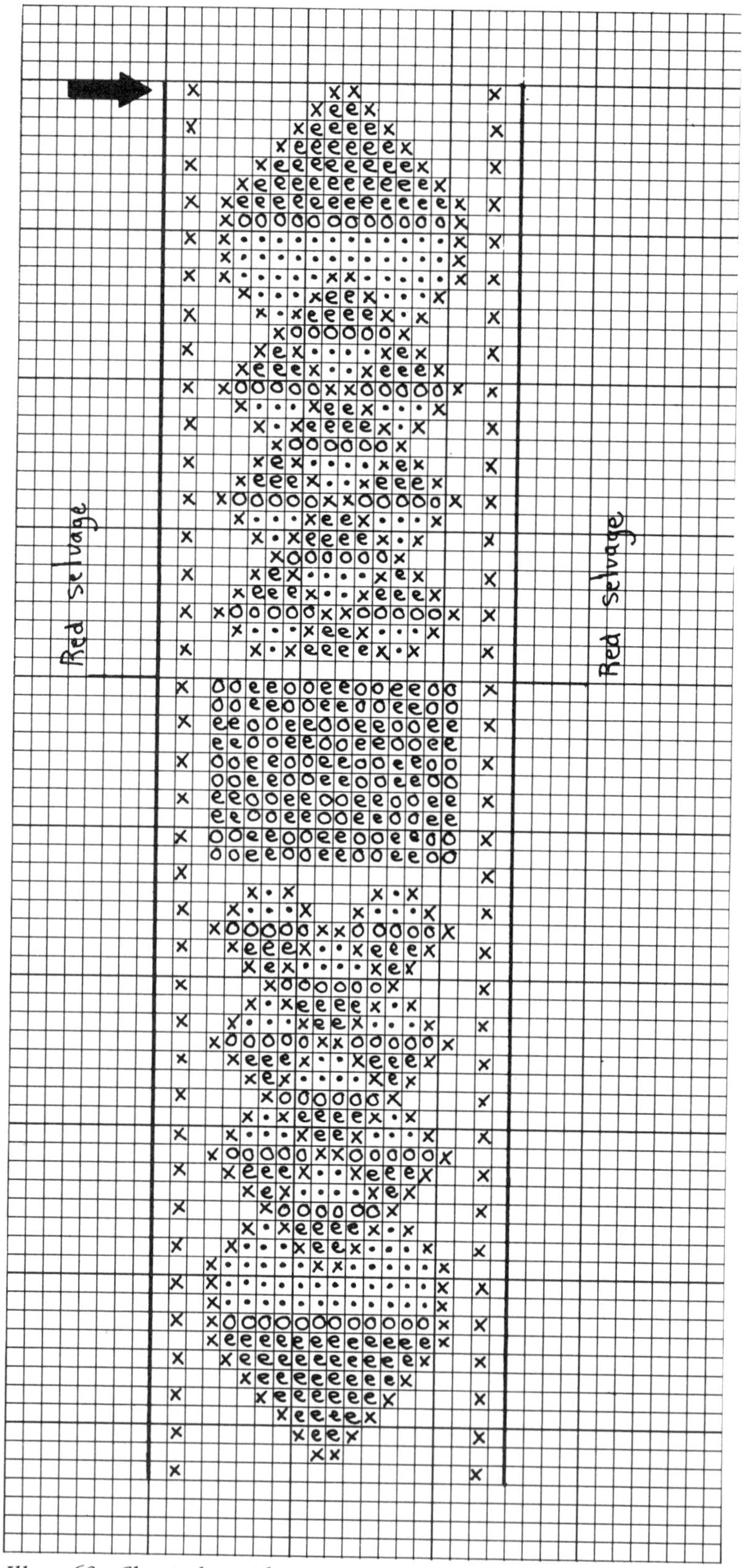

Illus. 63. Charted graph.

Hearts and Diamonds (Bookmark)

Degree of work: simple
Fabric: linen Skandia Band, 20-thread count,
ecru, 2" wide
Cut size of cloth needed: 13" long
Finished size: approximately 2" wide × 10 1/8"

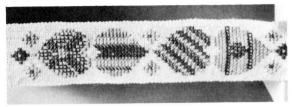

In color page D.

Cross-Stitch Key

Symbol	Color	J. & P. Coats six-strand floss	or DMC six-strand
⊠	46-B Beauty Rose		962
⊙	38 Dk. Orange		741
·	143 Lt. Cardinal		815
e	239 Imperial Blue		995
☐	Cloth as is		

Making the first cross-stitch: Measure 1" from top folded edge of linen. Start sewing at arrow.

Finishing directions

1. Repeat Steps 1–3 in "Hearts, Diamonds, and Checks." The only exception is: At Step 3 the measurement is 1".

Backstitch Key

Symbol	Color	J. & P. Coats six-strand floss	or DMC six-strand
	143 Lt. Cardinal		815
	46-B Beauty Rose		962
	239 Imperial Blue		995

Area of Backstitch: 143 Lt. Cardinal—Heart number 1 (at top) and 4 (at bottom). *46-B Beauty Rose*—Heart number 2. *239 Imperial Blue*—Heart number 3.

Purchase one skein of each color.

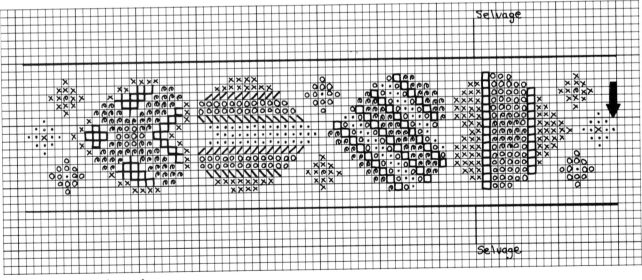

Illus. 64. Charted graph.

53

Guest Hand Towel

Degree of work: simple
Fabric: maxi-weave Ribband, 14-count, white with yellow edging, 1 7/8" wide
Cut size of cloth needed: 5/8" yard
Finished size: approximately 1 7/8" wide × 16"

Cross-Stitch Key

	J. & P. Coats six-strand floss	or DMC six-strand
Symbol	**Color**	
⊡	62 Russet	435
⊡	37 Dk. Lavender	554
⊟	223 Sun Gold	743
③	109 Dk. Willow Green	367
△	253 Daffodil	444
■	59-B Dk. Rose	899
⊠	46-A Mid Rose	3326
☐	Cloth as is	

Purchase one skein of each color.

Making the first cross-stitch: Measure 3" from left end of horizontal band. Start sewing at arrow.

Other materials: Yellow hand towel, 100% cotton—16 1/2" wide × 27 1/4". White pregathered cotton eyelet ruffle, 1 1/2" wide—5/8 yard.

Finishing directions

1. Cross-stitch up two and over two squares of fabric so 14 count is reduced to 7 stitches per inch.
2. With right sides up, place ruffle 1/4" from bottom of towel. Cut ruffle to width of towel, but at start and finish, add an additional 1/4" to turn back raw edges. Press back 1/4" on ends. Machine-stitch the ruffle to towel just below ruffle heading (Illus. 65).

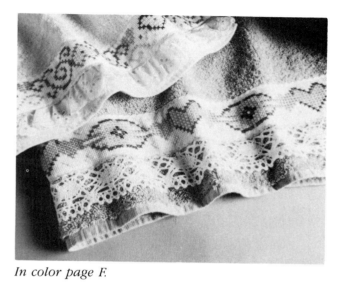

In color page F.

3. With right sides up, center Ribband over and covering ruffle heading. Fold Ribband ends towards back of towel. Press. Beyond pressed folds add additional 1 1/4" seam allowances. Cut off excess Ribband. Press back 1/4" on ends (Illus. 66).

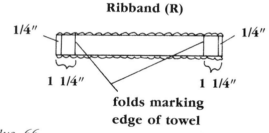

Ribband (R)

1/4"   1/4"

1 1/4"   1 1/4"

folds marking edge of towel

Illus. 66.

4. With right sides up, place Ribband over ruffle heading; arrange ends on towel back. Machine-stitch along top and bottom edges. Stitch just inside yellow edging (Illus. 67).

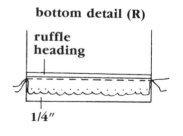

bottom detail (R)

ruffle heading

1/4"

Illus. 65.

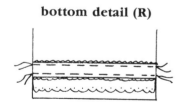

bottom detail (R)

Illus. 67.

5. On back of towel slipstitch folded ends of Rib-band (Illus. 68).

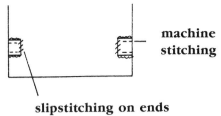

machine stitching

slipstitching on ends

Illus. 68.

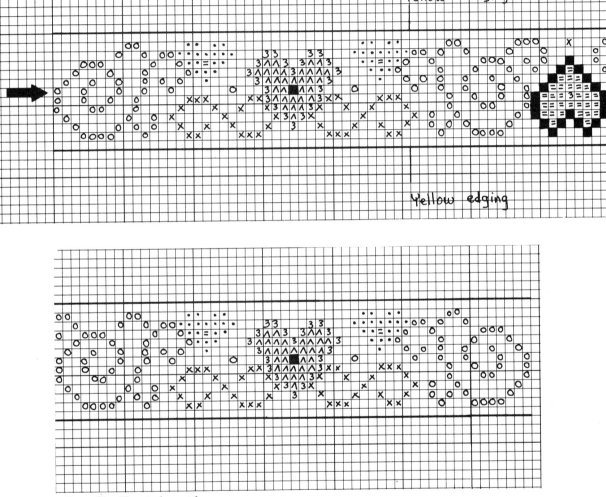

Illus. 69. Charted graph.

Tulips and Hearts (Potholder)

Degree of work: simple
Fabric: aida 8, white
Cut size of cloth needed: 13" square
Finished size: approximately 9" square without ruffle

Cross-Stitch Key

	J. & P. Coats six-strand floss	or DMC six-strand
Symbol	**Color**	
⊠	108 Steel Blue	792
⊟	253 Daffodil	444
⊙	140 Signal Red	321
ⓔ	62 Russet	435
•	99 Grass Green	703
ⓢ	46-A Mid Rose	3326
△	38-B Tangerine	947
☐	Cloth as is	

Backstitch Key

	J. & P. Coats six-strand floss	or DMC six-strand
Symbol	**Color**	
⌐	62 Russet	435

Area of Backstitch: *62 Russet*—Two small lines in tulips.

Purchase one skein of each color.

Making the first cross-stitch: Measure across 3 1/2" from top left corner; measure downwards 3 1/8" from top left corner. Mark point where two measurements intersect. Start sewing at arrow.

Other materials: Prequilted blue and white gingham, for back—12" square. White cotton for lining—12" square. White pregathered cotton eyelet ruffle—1 1/4" wide × 40". 1" plastic ring.

Finishing directions

1. Add 1 1/8" borders to all sides of design. Using knotted single strand of white thread, hand-stitch these lines by following one row in aida and by weaving in and out cloth with 1" running stitches (Illus. 70).

In color page F.

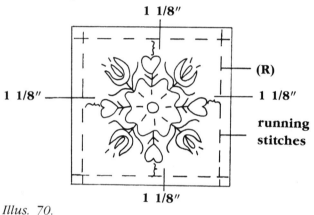

Illus. 70.

2. Place lining over wrong side back. Pin.

3. With right sides together, add ruffle to embroidered front. Start in middle of one side and turn back end 1/4". Baste so bottom of ruffle heading rests on running stitches. Overlap ends by 1"; turn back end 1/4". (Illus. 71).

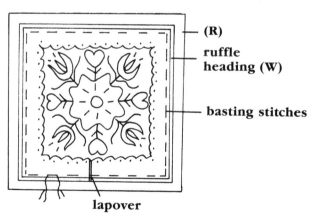

Illus. 71.

56

4. With right sides together, place front over back/lining. Pin. Machine-stitch, pivoting at corners. Sew right on running stitches. Leave 3″ opening in middle of one side.

5. Trim seams to 1/2″. Turn. Press fabric at opening inwards.

6. To hang, sew plastic ring to back (Illus. 72). Place in corner behind pink tulip and below quilted edges.

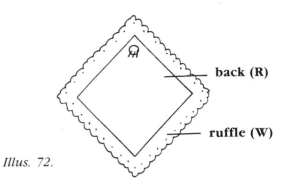

Illus. 72.

back (R)

ruffle (W)

Illus. 73. Charted graph.

Hearts in a Star (Potholder)

Degree of work: simple
Fabric: aida 8, white
Cut size of cloth needed: 13" square
Finished size: approximately 9" square without ruffle

Cross-Stitch Key

Symbol	J. & P. Coats six-strand floss Color	or DMC six-strand
⊠	108 Steel Blue	792
=	253 Daffodil	444
o	140 Signal Red	321
e	62 Russet	435
·	99 Grass Green	703
s	46-A Mid Rose	3326
△	38-B Tangerine	947
☐	Cloth as is	

Backstitch Key

Symbol	J. & P. Coats six-strand floss Color	or DMC six-strand
⊞	140 Signal Red	321
	99 Grass Green	703
	108 Steel Blue	792

Area of Backstitch: *140 Signal Red*—Inner square and three lines at top of each flower. *99 Grass Green*—Leaf stems. *108 Steel Blue*—Outlines within each flower.

Purchase one skein of each color.

Making the first cross-stitch: Measure across 3 1/4" from top left corner; measure downwards 3 1/4" from top left corner. Mark point where two measurements intersect. Start sewing at arrow.

In color page F.

Other materials: Prequilted blue and white gingham for back—12" square. White cotton, for lining—12" square. White pregathered cotton eyelet ruffle—1 1/4" wide × 40". 1" plastic ring.

Finishing directions
Repeat Steps 1–6 in "Tulips and Hearts." The only exception is: At Step 1 the measurement is 1" (Illus. 74).

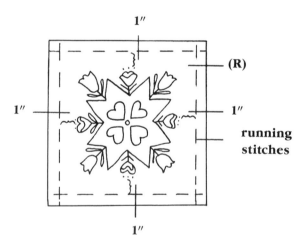

Illus. 74.

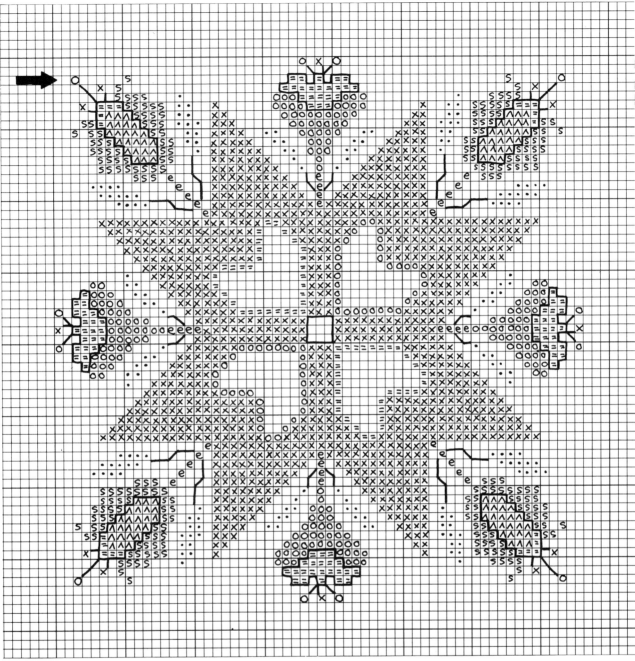

Illus. 75. Charted graph.

Belt

Degree of work: simple
Fabric: linen Skandia Band, 20-thread count, ecru, 2" wide
Cut size of cloth needed: 1 5/8 yards
Finished size: approximately 23 1/2" of embroidery centered on 1 5/8 yards

Cross-Stitch Key

Symbol	J. & P. Coats six-strand floss	or DMC six-strand
Symbol	Color	
◻O◻	12 Black	310
•	46-B Beauty Rose	962
⊠	239 Imperial Blue	995
e	8 Blue	800
■	143 Lt. Cardinal	815
◻	Cloth as is	

Backstitch Key

Symbol	J. & P. Coats six-strand floss	or DMC six-strand
Symbol	Color	
⌐	12 Black	310

Area of Backstitch: *12 Black*—Outline around light blue hearts.

Purchase two skeins of 46-B Beauty Rose. Buy one skein of each remaining color.

Making the first cross-stitch: See Step 3. Then start sewing at arrow.

Finishing directions

1. Finish off ends of linen. With right sides up, turn back 1/2"; press. Turn under 1/4" on raw edges. Press. Slipstitch folded inner edges (Illus. 76).

In color page D.

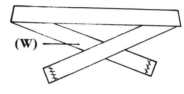

Illus. 76.

2. Check to see that design fits your waist. Cut piece of string 58 1/2" long; fold in half. Mark center. From center measure a mark 11 3/4" on either side. Tie string around your waist; even up ends. Knot once in front. Decide if there is too little or too much embroidery. If too little, sew one more repeat. Each repeat is approximately 3 1/8" long and consists of two large hearts facing each other with a pair of blue hearts in between (Illus. 77).

3 1/8"

one repeat

Illus. 77.

If too much, omit last repeat. If changes are made, recenter embroidery by adding or substracting equal measurements from belts ends.

3. If no design changes are made, measure 16 3/4" from left end of horizontally held belt. Do embroidery.

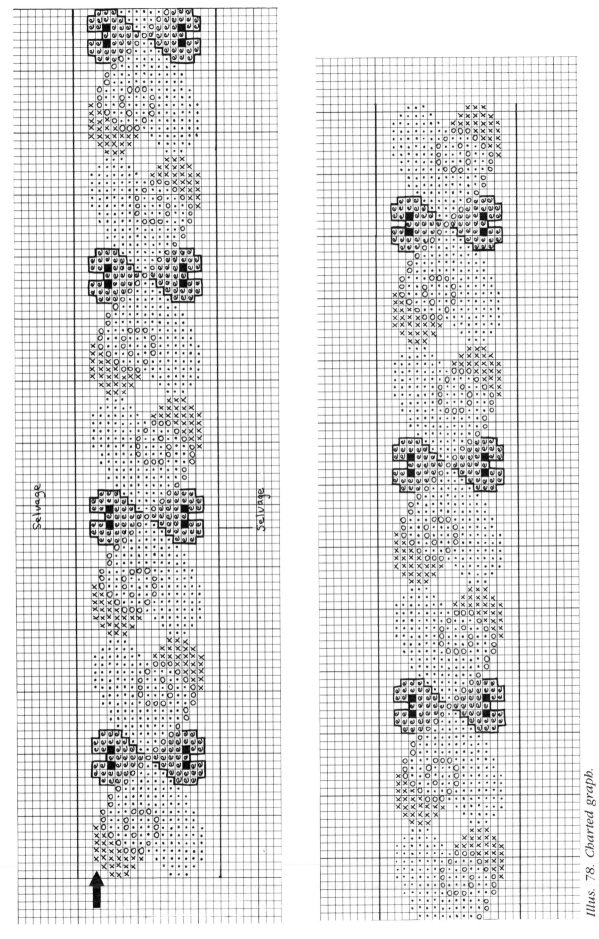

Selvage

Selvage

Illus. 78. Charted graph.

61

Bread Cloth

Degree of work: simple
Fabric: aida 8, white
Cut size of cloth needed: 20" square
Finished size: approximately 16" wide × 15 3/4"

Cross-Stitch Key

Symbol	J. & P. Coats six-strand floss Color	or DMC six-strand
⊠	62 Russet	435
·	253 Daffodil	444
⊙	140 Signal Red	321
e	99 Grass Green	703
=	108 Steel Blue	792
☐	Cloth as is	

Purchase two skeins each of 62 Russet and 253 Daffodil. Buy one skein of each remaining color.

Making the first cross-stitch: Measure across 3" from top left corner; measure downwards 3" from top left corner. Mark point where two measurements intersect. Start sewing at arrow.

Other materials: Red and white gingham, for back—18" square.

Finishing directions

1. Add 1" borders to all sides of design. Mark measurements with pins. Then using knotted single strand of white thread, hand-stitch these lines by following one row in aida and by weaving in and out cloth with 1" running stitches (Illus. 79).

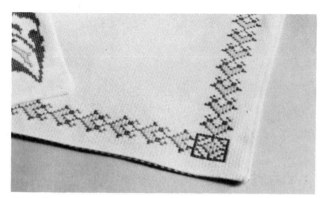

In color page B.

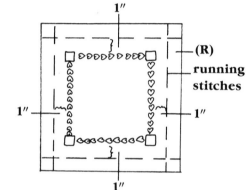

Illus. 79.

2. With right sides together center front over back. Pin. Machine-stitch, pivoting at corners. Sew right on running stitches, leaving 3" opening in middle of one side.

3. Trim seams to 1/2". Turn. Press fabric at opening inwards.

4. Machine-topstitch 1/8" from edges of cloth.

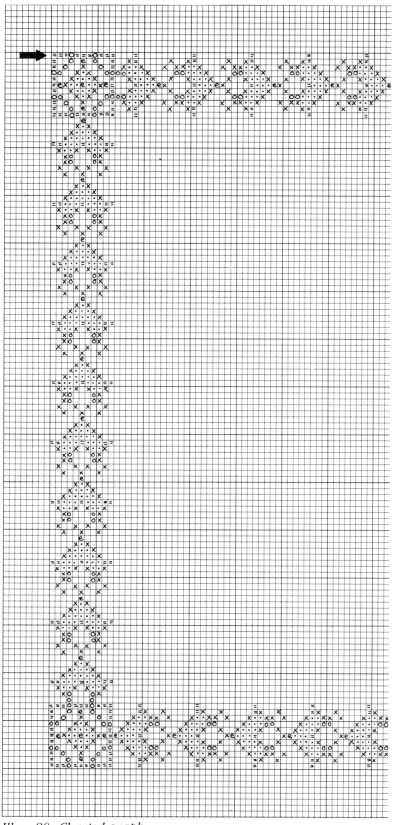

Illus. 80. Charted graph.

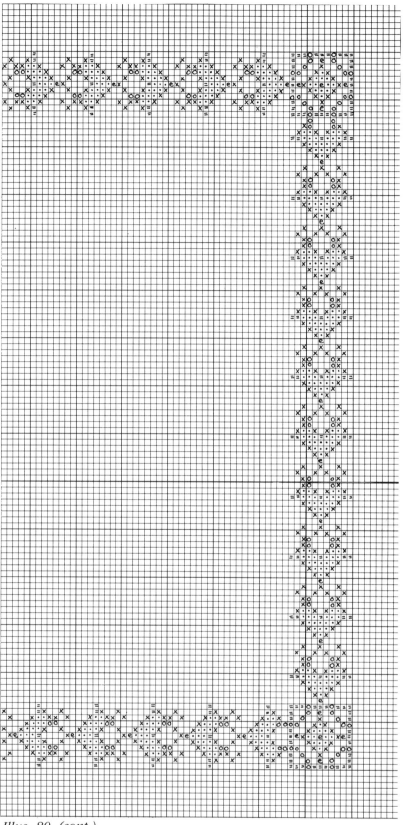

Illus. 80. (cont.).

Photo Album Cover

Degree of work: simple
Fabric: aida 8, white
Cut size of cloth needed: 30" wide × 18"
Finished size: approximately 8" wide × 8 1/2" of embroidery centered on 10 1/2" wide × 12" album

Cross-Stitch Key

Symbol	J. & P. Coats six-strand floss Color	or DMC six-strand
⊠	231 Goldenrod	742
⊙	245 Atlantic Blue	799
e	10-A Canary Yellow	445
■	248 Bright Avocado	906
◹	75-A Tropic Orange	920
=	81-A Colonial Brown	433
◆	132-A Parakeet	996
☐	Cloth as is	

Purchase two skeins of 231 Goldenrod. Buy one skein of each remaining color.

Making the first cross-stitch: Measure across 16" from top left corner; measure downwards 4 1/2" from top edge. Mark point where two measurements intersect (Illus. 81). Start sewing at arrow.

Other materials: Gold cotton for back—18" wide × 30". White cotton, for lining—18" wide × 30". Photo album, spiral ring—10 1/4" wide × 11 3/4" high × 1 1/8" deep. Masking tape.

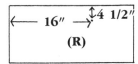

Illus. 81. Intersection of two measurements.

Finishing directions

1. With right sides up, center embroidery over album cover. Get side borders equal (mine are 1 3/4"); get top and bottom borders equal (mine are 1 3/8"). Mark measurements with pins, but add an additional 1/8" to each edge. Using knotted single strand of white thread, hand-stitch these lines by following one row in aida and by weaving in and out cloth with running stitches (Illus. 82).

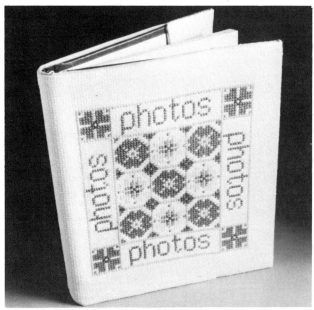

In color page D.

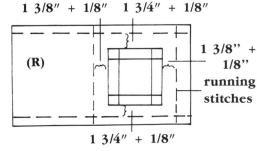

Illus. 82.

2. With wrong sides up, place back flat; place lining on top. Pin together.
3. With right sides together pin front over back/ lining. Machine-stitch at top and bottom (Illus. 83). Sew right on running stitches.
4. Trim two seams to 5/8". Turn. Press.

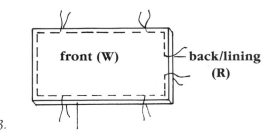

Illus. 83.

5. Center cover over album; fold flaps in at front and back. Mark folds with pins. Press lines into fabric. If flaps are more than 4" wide, cut off excess fabric.

6. Turn album cover wrong side out again. With pencil and ruler, lightly mark off 5/8″ seams on either end. Machine-stitch sides, leaving 3″ opening in middle of back (Illus. 84).

7. Cut fabric at corners on slant to reduce bulk. Turn. Press fabric at opening inward. Slipstitch opening.

8. Center cover over album, folding flaps inside. Temporarily tape cover in position so you can slipstitch flaps at top and bottom (Illus. 85). Remove tape.

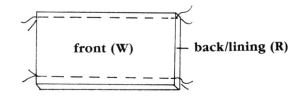

Illus. 84.

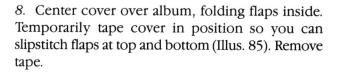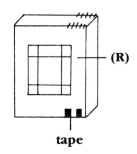

Illus. 85.

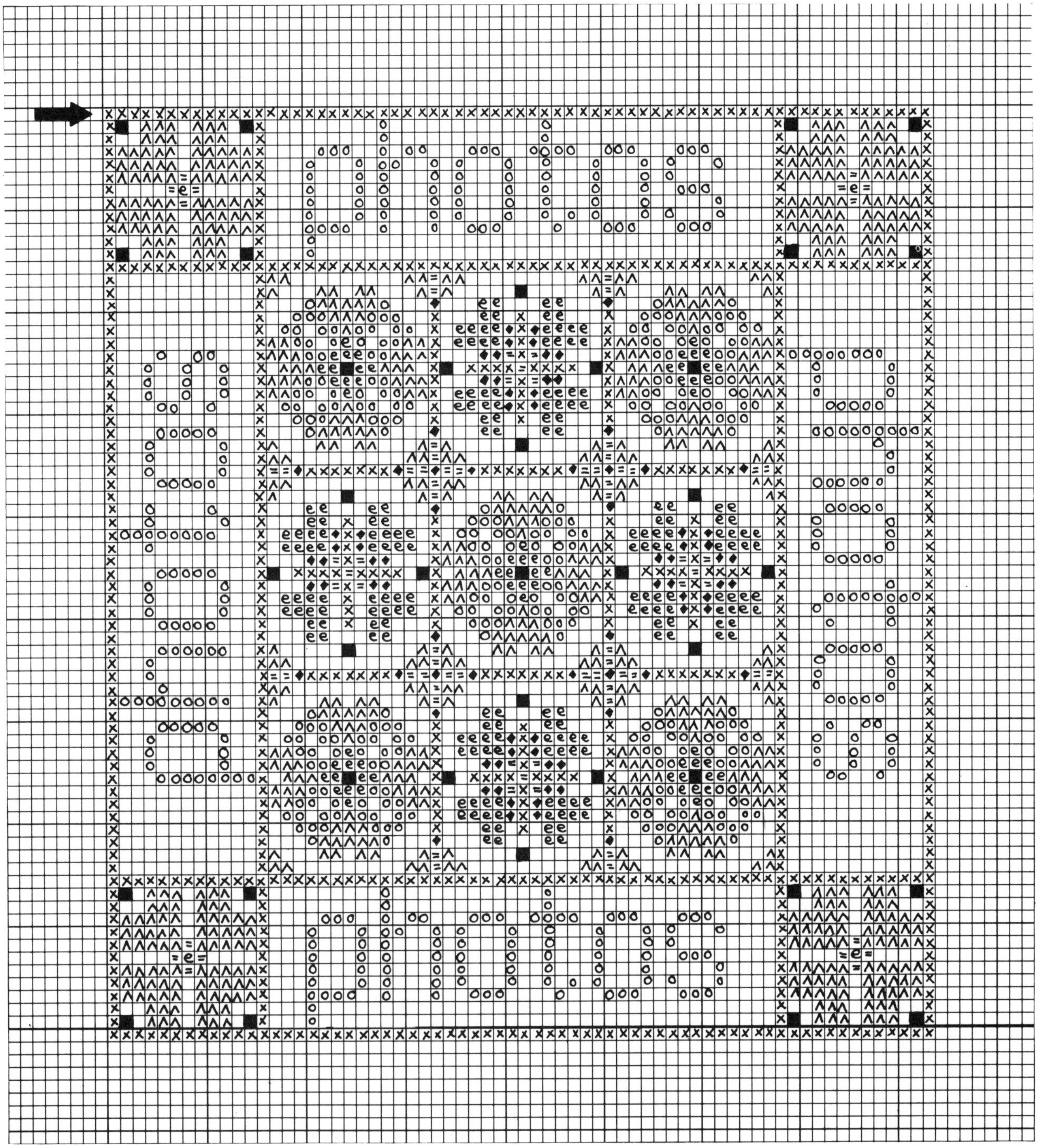

Illus. 86. Charted graph.

Pennsylvania Dutch (Handbag)

Degree of work: intermediate
Fabric: aida 11, ivory
Cut size of cloth needed: 12 1/2" wide × 11"
Finished size: approximately 9" wide × 7"

Cross-Stitch Key

Symbol	Color	J. & P. Coats six-strand floss	or DMC six-strand
⊡	140 Signal Red		321
⊙	62 Russet		435
⊠	91 Emerald Green		913
⊟	253 Daffodil		444
◺	132-A Parakeet		996
■	44 Royal Blue		796
◆	81-B Dk. Colonial Brown		801
☐	Cloth as is		

Backstitch Key

Symbol	Color	J. & P. Coats six-strand floss	or DMC six-strand
⊞	91 Emerald Green		913
	132-A Parakeet		996

Area of Backstitch: *91 Emerald Green*—Heart outline.
132-A Parakeet—Bird's beak and tail.

Purchase two skeins of 91 Emerald Green. Buy one skein of each remaining color.

Making the first cross-stitch: Measure across 3" from top left corner; measure downwards 2 1/2" from top left corner. Mark point where two measurements intersect. Start sewing at arrow.

Other materials: Ivory sailcloth, for back and lining—12" wide × 22". Ivory single-fold bias tape—21". All-purpose Velcro, white—5/8" wide × 5 1/2".

Finishing directions

1. Cut sailcloth as diagrammed (Illus. 87).
2. Press strap in half lengthwise. Then fold raw edges towards center; press. Machine-stitch along open side. (Illus. 88).

In color page B.

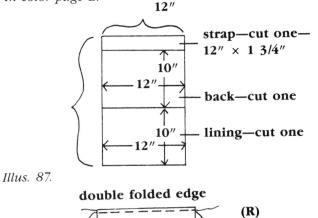

Illus. 87.

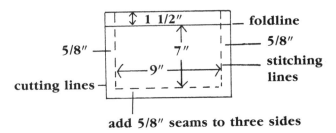

Illus. 88.

3. Make bag pattern (Illus. 89).
4. With right sides up, center front over lining. Pin. With right sides up, center pattern over front/lining. Arrange pattern so that you have 3/4" borders between embroidery and stitching lines and between embroidery and foldline. Pin. Cut. Transfer seams and foldline to wrong side front/lining.
5. Lay out and cut back. Transfer seams and foldline to wrong side.

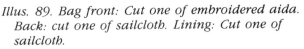

Illus. 89. Bag front: Cut one of embroidered aida. Back: cut one of sailcloth. Lining: Cut one of sailcloth.

6. With right sides together, place front/lining on back. Fold strap in half and wedge ends in left seam 7/8″ beneath foldline. Machine-stitch 3 sides, pivoting at corners (Illus. 90).

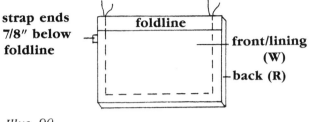

Illus. 90.

7. Trim 3 seams to 3/8″. Press side seams open. Turn.

8. Finish off top of bag. Center bias tape over raw edges. Pin. At end, lap over 1″ and turn tape back 1/4″. Machine-stitch close to bottom of tape (Illus. 91).

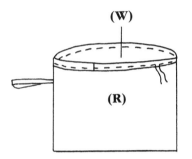

Illus. 91.

9. Turn bag in on foldline. Press. Slipstitch tape to inside of bag.

10. Center looped portion of Velcro inside back; position 1/4″ below foldline. Pin. Machine-stitch on all sides (Illus. 92).

11. Center fuzzy portion of Velcro inside front, 1/4″ below foldline. Pin. Machine-stitch on all sides.

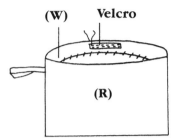

Illus. 92.

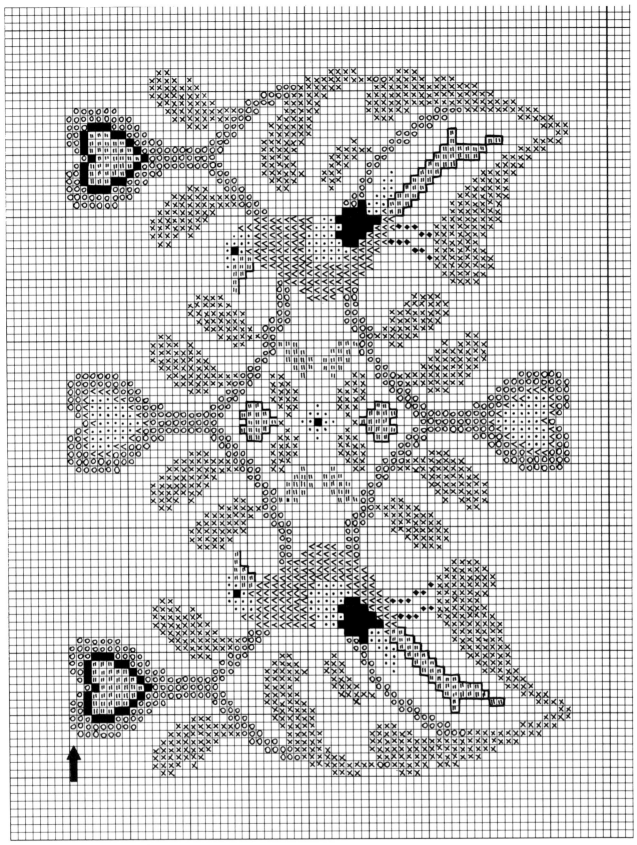

Illus. 93. Charted graph.

Tote Bag

Degree of work: intermediate
Fabric: linen Skandia Bands, 20-thread count,
ecru with red and brown selvages, 2 1/4" wide
Cut size of cloth needed: one with red selvages and
two with brown selvages—each 19" long
Finished size: three approximately 2 1/4" wide ×
12 1/2" strips centered on 12 1/2" square tote

Cross-Stitch Key

Symbol	J. & P. Coats six-strand floss	or DMC six-strand
	Color	
e	91 Emerald Green	913
⊠	38-B Tangerine	947
⧄	140 Signal Red	321
⊙	132-A Parakeet	996
·	81-A Colonial Brown	433
◺	36 Royal Purple	550
⊟	253 Daffodil	444
☐	Cloth as is	

Purchase three skeins of 132-A Parakeet. Buy one skein
of each remaining color.

Making the first cross-stitch: Measure 2″ from
top of each band. Start sewing at arrow.

Other materials: Ivory sailcloth, for front and
back—1/2 yard. Ivory cotton straps, 2″ wide ×
1 1/2 yards. Ivory single-fold bias tape—28″. Orange
jumbo rickrack—2 1/2 yards. Yellow baby rickrack—1 1/4 yards.

Finishing directions

1. Make tote pattern (Illus. 94).
2. Lay out and cut tote. Before pattern is unpinned,

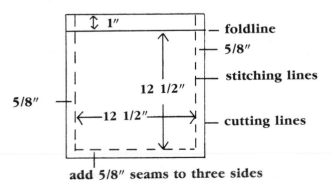

Illus. 94. Bag front: Cut one of sailcloth. Back: Cut
one of sailcloth.

In color page B.

transfer seams and foldline to wrong side of each
fabric.

3. On front and back, press foldline towards
wrong side of cloth.

4. With right sides up, place bands 1 and 3 on
front so brown selvages are 1 1/8″ away from side
stitching lines and start of embroidery rests on
foldline with ends extending entire length of front.
Pin. Place band 2 in middle so red selvages are
5 1/2″ from left stitching line and 4 3/4″ from right
stitching line (Illus. 95). Pin. Baste.

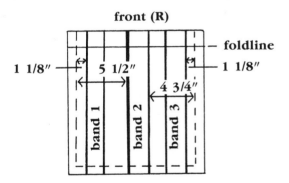

*** note: stitching lines and foldline are on right
side of front only to illustrate the measurements**

Illus. 95.

5. Add jumbo rickrack to front. Center one strip
between left stitching line and band 1 and between
band 3 and right stitching line. Rickrack extends
entire length front. Pin. Baste. Center two strips
between inner edges of band 1 and 2. Pin. Center
one strip between band 2 and 3. Pin.

6. Add baby rickrack to front. Center one strip on jumbos between bands 1 and 3. Pin. Baste.

7. Machine-stitch bands and rickrack to front. Stitch close to linen selvages. Stitch once down center of rickrack with orange thread.

8. With right sides together, stitch front to back, pivoting at corners. Press side seams open at top.

9. Finish off top of bag. Center bias tape over raw edges. Pin. At end lap over 1″, and turn tape back 1/4″. Machine-stitch close to bottom of tape (Illus. 96).

10. Turn tote in on foldline. Press. Slipstitch tape to inside of bag.

11. Cut straps in half; machine-stitch several times across raw ends. On front place one strap inside tote 1 1/2″ beneath foldline and in line with bands 1 and 3. Pin. Machine-stitch strap to tote by sewing a small rectangle at each end (Illus. 97). Position second strap inside back in same manner and in line with first.

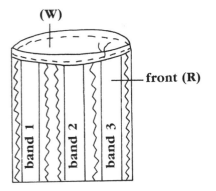

Illus. 96.

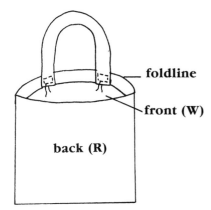

Illus. 97.

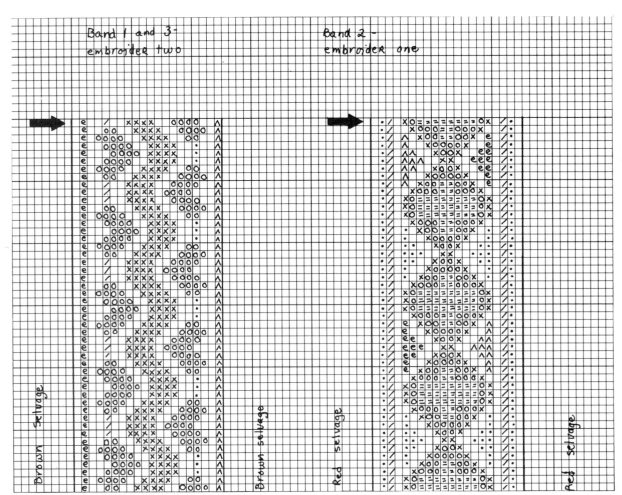

Illus. 98. Charted graph.

72

Illus. 98. (cont.).

Cat Table Runner

Degree of work: advanced
Fabric: aida 11, white
Cut size of cloth needed: 14 3/4" wide × 40"
Finished size: approximately 13 1/2" wide × 39"

In color page G.

Cross-Stitch Key

Symbol	J. & P. Coats six-strand floss Color	or DMC six-strand
■	100 Fast Red	816
3	253 Daffodil	444
T	37 Dk. Lavender	554
U	32 Purple	552
◆	12 Black	310
S	81-A Colonial Brown	433
e	24-A Oriental Blue	518
∧	9 Yellow	745
c	75-A Tropic Orange	920
L	38 Dk. Orange	741
◻	216 Avocado	469
∕	26 Nile Green	966
=	46-A Mid Rose	3326
✕	62 Russet	435
☐	Cloth as is	

Backstitch Key

Symbol	J. & P. Coats six-strand floss Color	or DMC six-strand
⊞	12 Black	310
	216 Avocado	469

Area of Backstitch: *12 Black*—Wings and antennae on butterfly; wing on bird; petal lines in flowers; all leaf veins; lines around cat's eyes, ears, face, upper paw, and hind leg; and cat's whiskers and claws. *216 Avocado*— All stems.

Purchase two skeins each of 75-A Tropic Orange, 216 Avocado, and 62 Russet. Buy one skein of each remaining color.

Making the first cross-stitch: See Step 4. Start sewing at arrow.

Finishing directions

1. Finish off edges of runner. Measure 5/8" seams on all sides of cloth; mark with pins. Then using knotted single strand of white thread, hand-stitch these lines by following one row in aida and by weaving in and out cloth with 1" running stitches (Illus. 99).

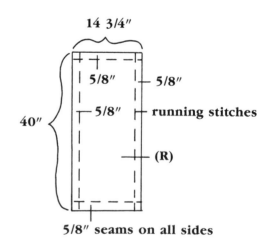

Illus. 99.

2. On sides, press back 5/8" seams. On top and bottom press back 5/8" seams. On sides turn under 1/4" on raw edges, fold towards running stitches. Press. On top and bottom turn under 1/4" on raw edges. Press.

3. Machine-stitch close to folded inner edges, pivoting at corners.

4. At bottom left side of runner, count in 5 squares on aida. Mark with pin. Using knotted single strand of thread, hand-stitch a 13″ line by following one row in aida and by weaving in and out cloth with 1″ running stitches. Then from bottom of runner, count up 138 squares. Make line of running stitches just above 138th square. Start cross-stitching butterfly's wing right beneath this line; refer to charted design for correct position from stitched vertical line on left (Illus. 100).

5. Turn runner upside down. Repeat Step 4. Do embroidery.

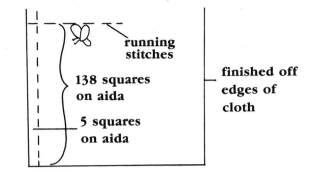

Illus. 100.

Illus. 101. Charted graph.

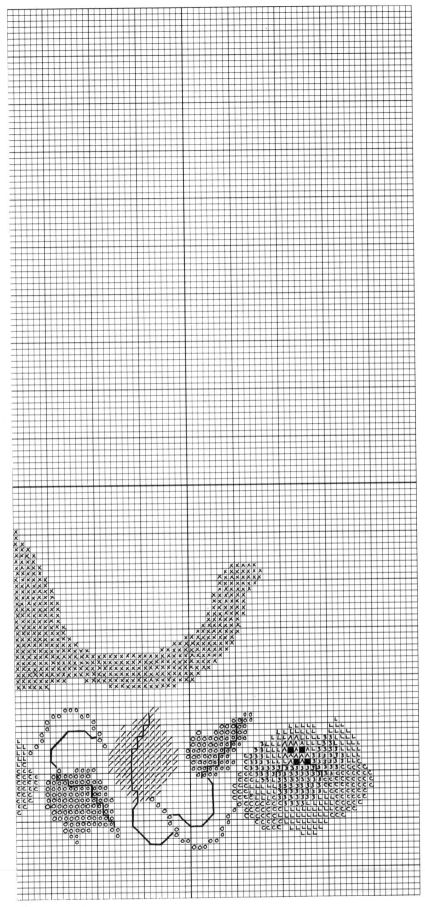

Illus. 101. (cont.).

Love and Romance

Bridal Hand and Bath Towels

Degree of work: simple
Fabric: maxi-weave Ribband, 14-count, white with blue edging, 1 7/8" wide
Cut size of cloth needed: 1 3/8 yards for set. Hand uses a 19" strip, bath towel uses 30 1/2"
Finished size: approximately 14 5/8" of embroidery on hand and 24 1/2" on bath towel

In color page F.

Cross-Stitch Key

	J. & P. Coats six-strand floss	or DMC six-strand
Symbol	**Color**	
⊙	100 Fast Red	816
·	69 Lt. Steel Blue	809
=	1 White	Snow-White
■	71 Pewter Grey	415
3	216 Avocado	469
S	26 Nile Green	966
△	223 Sun Gold	743
◆	12 Black	310
⊠	46-A Mid Rose	3326
☐	Cloth as is	

Purchase two skeins of 46-A Mid Rose. Buy one skein of each remaining color.

Making the first cross-stitch: On hand towel, measure 2" from left end of horizontal band. On bath towel measure 2 3/4" from left. Start sewing at arrow.

Other materials: Blue hand towel, 100% cotton—16" wide × 25 1/2". Bath towel, 100% cotton—25 1/2" wide × 47 1/4". White polyester flat lace, 1 5/8" wide—1 3/8 yards for set.

Finishing directions

1. Repeat Step 1 in "Guest Hand Towel."
2. With right sides up, place lace at bottom of both towels. At start and finish, turn back 1/2". Press. Turn under 1/4" on raw edge; press. Slipstitch folded edges of lace to prevent unravelling.
3. With right sides up, place lace on hand towel so that it is 1/4" from bottom edge; 3/4" from bottom of bath towel. Match sides. Machine-stitch lace to towel; stitch 1/8" from top edge (Illus. 102).
4. With right sides up, center Ribband over and covering stitching in top of lace. Repeat Steps 3-5 in "Guest Hand Towel."

bottom of towels

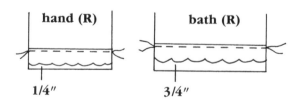

Illus. 102. Bottom of towels.

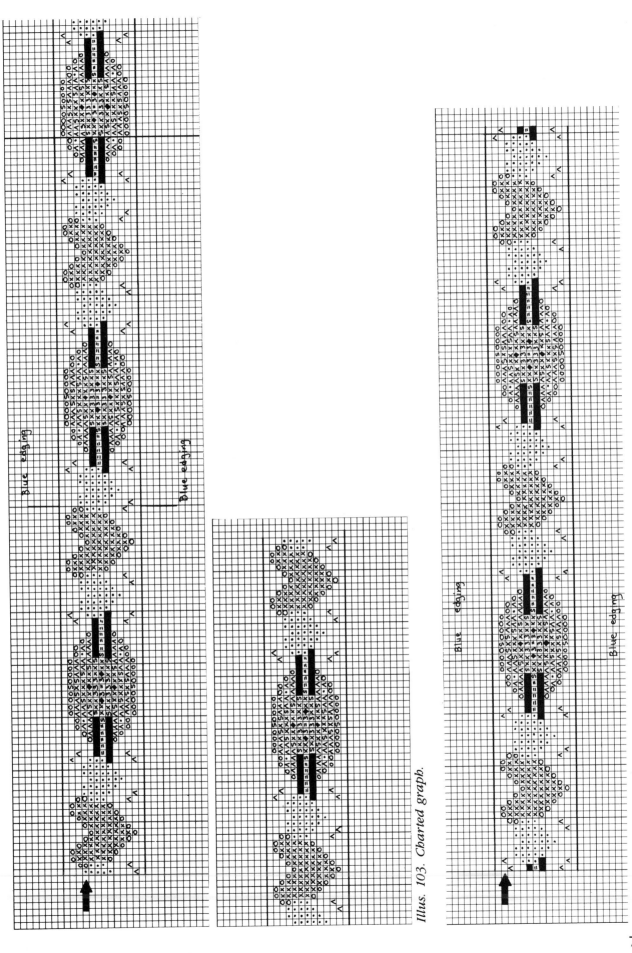

Illus. 103. Charted graph.

Illus. 104. Charted graph.

79

Box Lid

Degree of work: simple
Fabric: aida 11, white
Cut size of cloth needed: 11 1/2" wide × 10"
Finished size: approximately 5 5/8" wide × 4" of embroidery centered in 7" wide × 5" design area

Cross-Stitch Key

Symbol	J. & P. Coats six-strand floss Color	or DMC six-strand
⊠	248 Bright Avocado	906
◎	81 Dk. Brown	434
◺	65 Beauty Pink	605
⑤	32 Purple	552
⊟	46-B Beauty Rose	956
■	253 Daffodil	444
·	Use DMC color	369
⌊	Use DMC color	819
□	Cloth as is	

Backstitch Key

Symbol	J. & P. Coats six-strand floss Color	or DMC six-strand
	46-B Beauty Rose	956
	81 Dk. Brown	434

Area of Backstitch: 46-B Beauty Rose—Within five light pink diamonds. 81 Dk. Brown—Within three dark pink diamonds.

Purchase one skein of each color.

Making the first cross-stitch: Measure across 3" from top left corner; measure downwards 3" from top left corner. Mark point where two measurements intersect. Start sewing at arrow.

Other materials: Bleached muslin, for backing—10 1/2" wide × 8 1/2". Sudberry House Picture Frame Box (hinged, woodstain with 7" × 5" design area, style #99701). Masking tape. 8 small wire nails—1/2 × 19 flat head.

Finishing directions

1. Press out mounting and backing boards from box top.

In color page H.

2. Center muslin over *mounting board* (smallest). Fold in top and bottom, then sides. Tape (Illus. 105).

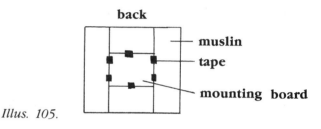

Illus. 105.

3. To embroidery add 7/8" borders on sides and 3/4" borders on top and bottom. Using knotted single strand of thread, hand-stitch these lines by following one row in aida and by weaving in and out cloth with 1" running stitches (Illus. 106).

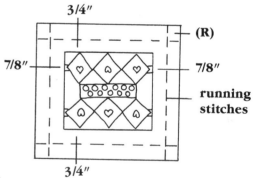

Illus. 106.

4. Beyond running stitches, add an additional 1 1/2" seam allowance on all sides. Cut off excess fabric.

5. Finish off edges of aida. Turn back 1/4" on all sides; press. Machine-stitch 1/8" from folded edges.

6. Repeat Steps 7–10 in "Mounting and Framing." The only exception is: At Step 7 you lay muslin/mounting board over the embroidery.

7. Place needlework inside box. Add backing board. To permanently hold everything in position, gently hammer two nails in each side of box. (Illus. 107).

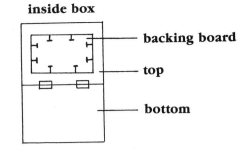

Illus. 107.

Illus. 108. Charted graph.

Doves (Lingerie Bag)

Degree of work: intermediate
Fabric: aida 11, ivory
Cut size of cloth needed: 16" wide × 36"
Finished size: approximately 10 3/4" wide × 10"

Cross-Stitch Key

Symbol	J. & P. Coats six-strand floss Color	or DMC six-strand
⊠	69 Lt. Steel Blue	809
·	9 Yellow	745
◹	253 Daffodil	444
■	218 Coral Glow	893
◿	51-C Gold Brown	436
⊙	81-A Colonial Brown	433
☐	Cloth as is	

Backstitch Key

Symbol	J. & P. Coats six-strand floss Color	or DMC six-strand
⊞	213 Beige	644

Area of Backstitch: 213 Beige—Decorative filling within the heart.

Purchase two skeins each of 69 Lt. Steel Blue and 213 Beige. Buy one skein of each remaining color.

Making the first cross-stitch: Measure 12 3/4" from left bottom edge; measure 6" from left edge. Mark point where two measurements intersect (Illus. 109). Start sewing at arrow.

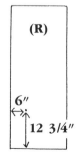

Illus. 109. Intersection of measurements.

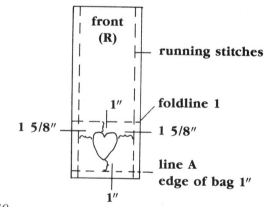

In color page G.

Areas of special concern: Initials change. See letters #3. There are 23 spaces available for bride's first and last initials. Leave 2 spaces between each letter. Start each pair of initials on left where "E" begins. Work details out on graph paper.

Other materials: Pale yellow polyester satin, for lining—14" wide × 34". Yellow satin ribbon, double-faced, 5/8" wide—1 1/8 yards.

Finishing directions

1. Add borders to embroidery. Measure 1" above and beneath heart and 1 5/8" on either side. Mark with pins. Using knotted single strand of beige thread, hand-stitch these lines by following one row in aida and by weaving in and out cloth with 1" running stitches (Illus. 110).

Illus. 110.

2. Sew two more lines on front. Measure 10 1/8″ above foldline 1; mark with pin. Sew foldline 2 parallel to foldline 1. Then measure 10 1/8″ above foldline 2; sew line B parallel also (Illus. 111).

3. Cut ribbon into 4 equal pieces.

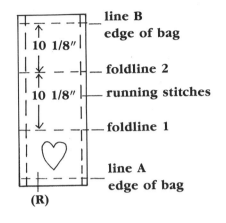

Illus. 111.

4. Pin 2 ribbons on right side front. Get outer edges of ribbon even with outer edges of initials. Extend ribbon ends 1/2″ beyond line A; baste (Illus. 112).

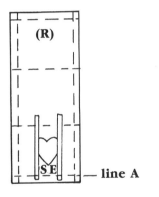

Illus. 112.

5. With right sides together, place front over lining. Pin with ribbons wedged in between. Machine-stitch, pivoting at corners. Sew right on running stitches. Leave 3″ opening in middle of one side (Illus. 113).

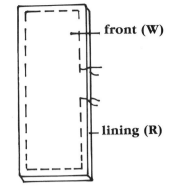

Illus. 113.

6. Trim seams to 1/2″. Turn. Press fabric at opening inwards. Slipstitch opening.

7. Press bag inwards on foldlines 1 and 2.

8. With embroidered flap lifted out of way, pin sides of bag. Press back 3/8″ on one of each remaining ribbon; fold and press back another 3/8″ so raw edges are completely hidden. Pin finished ends of ribbon on back of bag 3/8″ above foldline 2. Check also to see that ribbons are in line with those on front. Machine-stitch 3 sides, pivoting at corners and catching ribbon ends as well (Illus. 114 and 115).

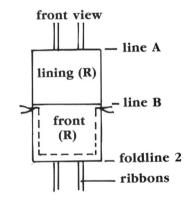

Illus. 114.

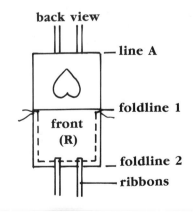

Illus. 115.

Illus. 116. Charted graph.

Serving Tray

Degree of work: intermediate
Fabric: aida 11, ivory
Cut size of cloth needed: 15" wide × 12"
Finished size: approximately 8 1/2" wide × 5 7/8"
centered in 10" wide × 7" design area

Cross-Stitch Key

Symbol	J. & P. Coats six-strand floss Color	or DMC six-strand
O	81 Dk. Brown	434
=	120 Crimson	351
⊠	98 Fern Green	989
△	11 Orange	972
S	143 Lt. Cardinal	815
■	109 Dk. Willow Green	367
·	61 Ecru	822
□	Cloth as is	

Backstitch Key

Symbol	J. & P. Coats six-strand floss Color	or DMC six-strand
⊞	81-B Dk. Colonial Brown	801

Area of Backstitch: *81-B Dk. Colonial Brown—All.*

Purchase one skein of each color.

Making the first cross-stitch: Measure across 3" from top left corner; measure downwards 3" from top left corner. Mark point where two measurements intersect. Start sewing at arrow.

Other materials: Sudberry House Petite Serving Tray (woodstain with 10" × 7" rectangle mat, style #65651). Stitch Witchery—15" wide × 12".

In color page C.

Finishing directions

1. Add Stitch Witchery to wrong side of embroidery. Follow manufacturer's instructions for bonding.

2. Remove screws at one end of tray. Slide out wooden mat, cardboard, and base. Glass is inside. Handle with care; clean.

3. Place tracing paper over cardboard. Trace rectangular shape. With right sides up center tracing over needlework/Stitch Witchery. Get borders equal at sides (mine are about 1 3/4") and at top and bottom (mine are about 1 1/2"). Pin tracing to needlework. Cut fabric same size as cardboard.

4. With right sides up, tape needlework to cardboard in a north-south-east-west position.

5. Reassemble frame. Working from bottom to top, slide in base (wrong side up), needlework/cardboard combination (right side up), wooden mat (right side up), and glass on top.

6. Replace end of tray.

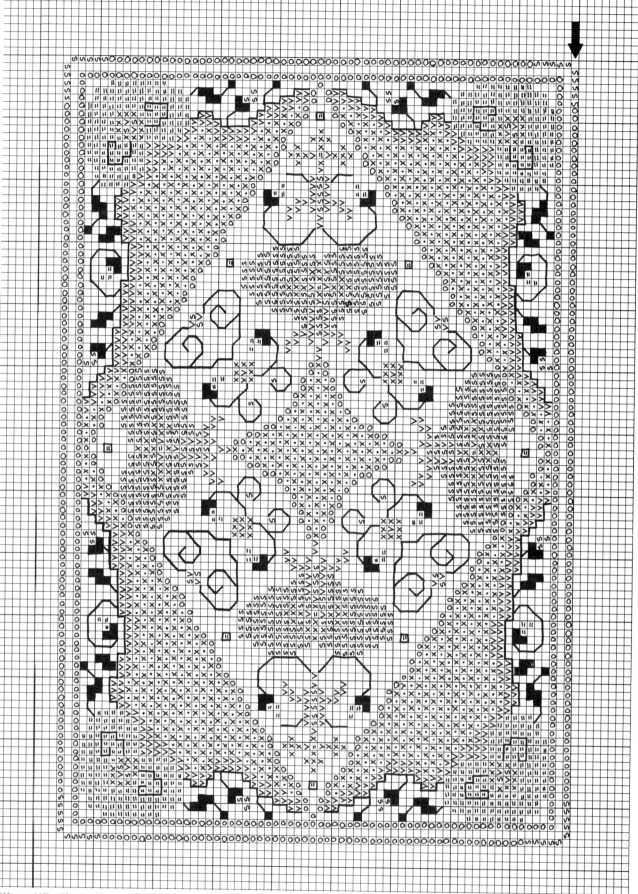

Illus. 117. Charted graph.

Dresser Scarf

Degree of work: advanced
Fabric: cork linen, 19-thread count, pink
Cut size of cloth needed: 16 1/2″ wide × 36″
Finished size: approximately 14 1/2″ wide × 34″

Cross-Stitch Key

Symbol	J. & P. Coats six-strand floss	or DMC six-strand
	Color	
L	65 Beauty Pink	776
e	1 White	Snow-White
⊠	51-C Gold Brown	436
◁	81-B Dk. Colonial Brown	801
=	26 Nile Green	966
·	28-B Treeleaf Green	991
◯	46-B Beauty Rose	962
♥	223 Sun Gold	743
T	59-C Jewel Rose	309
S	260 Maple Wood	437
╱	124 Indian Pink	353
◆	10-A Canary Yellow	445
■	248 Bright Avocado	906
▣	252 Chinese Yellow	307
☐	Cloth as is	

Backstitch Key

Symbol	J. & P. Coats six-strand floss	or DMC six-strand
	Color	
	140 Signal Red	321
	81-B Dk. Colonial Brown	801

Area of Backstitch: *140 Signal Red*—Surrounding all yellow dots on flowers and large buds. *81-B Dk. Colonial Brown*—Within all flowers, at ends of large buds, and stems.

Purchase two skeins each of 28-B Treeleaf Green, 46-B Beauty Rose, and 124 Indian Pink. Buy one skein of each remaining color.

In color page H.

Making the first cross-stitch: Measure across 5 1/2″ from top left corner; measure downwards 3″ from top left corner. Mark point where two measurements intersect. Start sewing at arrrow.

Other materials: Pink cotton, for back—16″ wide × 36″. White pregathered polyester eyelet ruffle, 1 1/4″ wide—2 3/4 yards.

Finishing directions

1. Make dresser-scarf pattern. To do, transfer end pattern (Illus. 118) to left side of large sheet of tracing paper, add measurements in center, and at right repeat end as diagrammed (Illus. 119).

2. With pattern centered over linen, lay out and cut front. Transfer stitching lines to wrong side cloth. Repeat same procedure for cotton back.

3. With right sides together, add ruffle to front. Start in middle of one side, begin by turning back 1/2″. Baste so bottom of ruffle heading rests on lines transferred to wrong side front. Overlap ends by 2″; turn back last 1/2″ (Illus. 120).

4. With right sides together and stitching lines matching, stitch front to back with ruffle wedged in between. Leave 4″ opening along middle of one side. Trim seams to 1/2″.

5. Turn. Press fabric at opening inwards. Slipstitch opening.

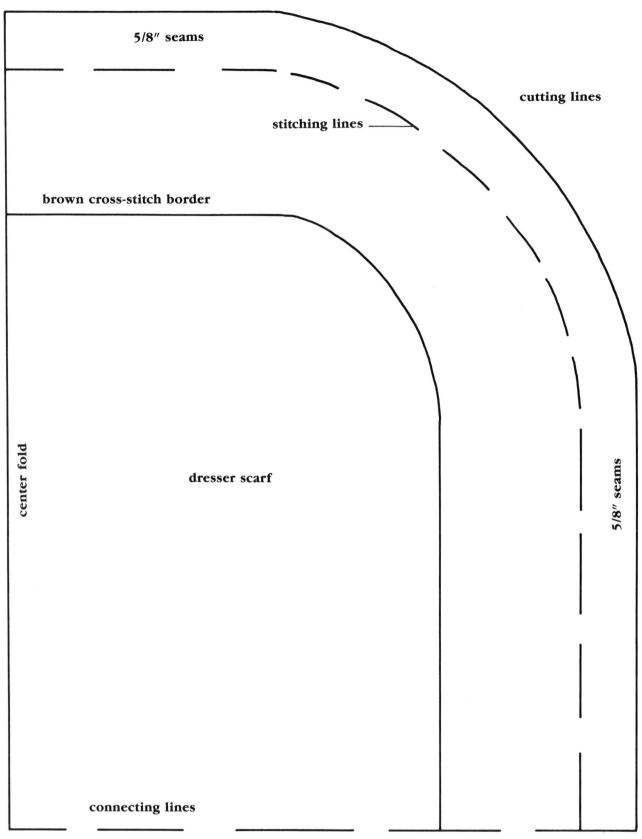

Illus. 118. End pattern.

add 5/8″ seams here

end
pattern

center
fold

16 1/4″   13″

end
pattern

center
fold

add 5/8″ seams here

*Illus. 119. Dresser scarf front: Cut one of
embroidered linen. Back: Cut one of pink cotton.*

front (R)

ruffle
heading

ruffle (W)

overlap

Illus. 120.

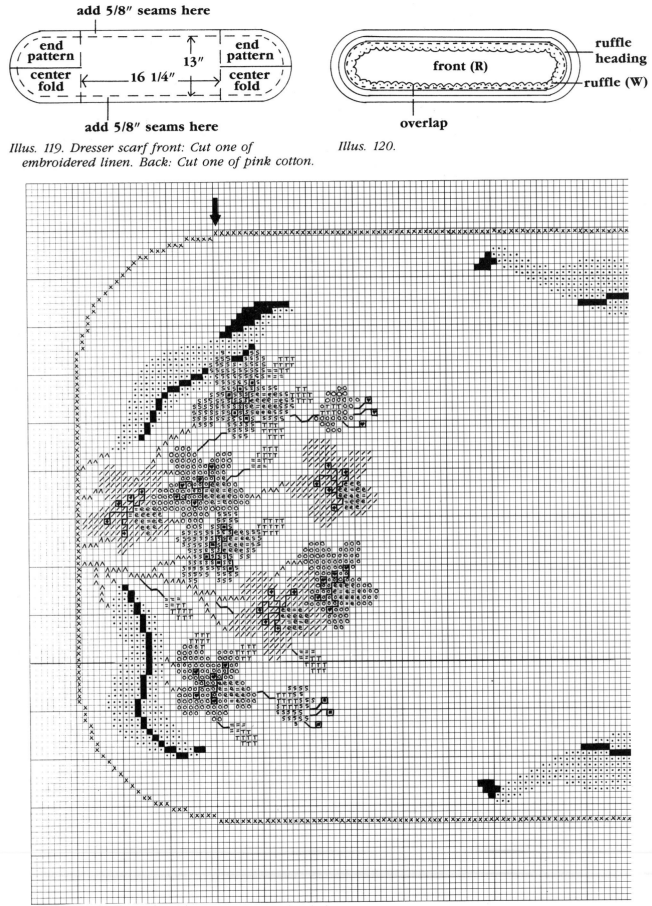

Illus. 121. Charted graph.

Illus. 121. (cont.).

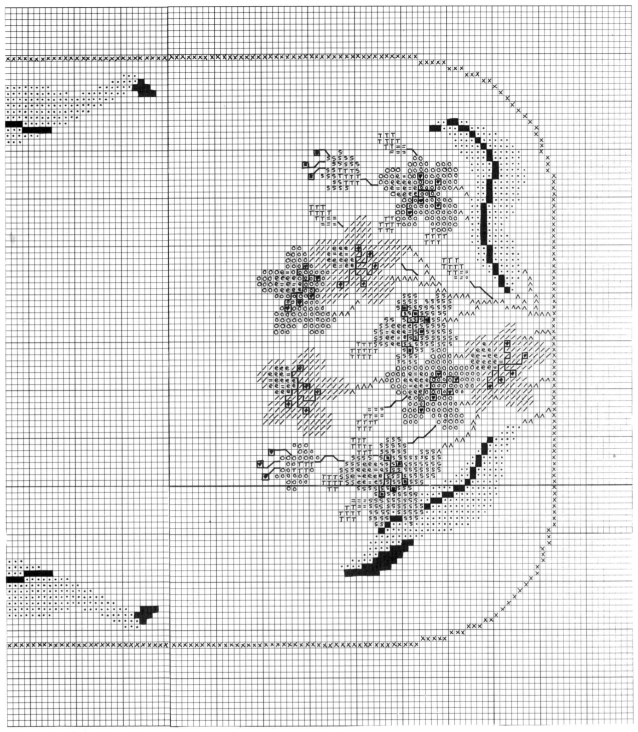

Illus. 121. (cont.).

Bridal Pillowcases 1 and 2

Degree of work: advanced
Fabric: aida 11, ivory
Cut size of cloth needed: 16" square for each
Finished size: approximately 12 1/2" wide × 12"
of embroidery centered on each standard case

Cross-Stitch Key

Symbol	J. & P. Coats six-strand floss	or DMC six-strand
	Color	
L	223 Sun Gold	743
△	69 Lt. Steel Blue	809
=	46-A Mid Rose	3326
■	132-A Parakeet	996
U	81-A Colonial Brown	433
e	122 Watermelon	961
O	4-A Mid Pink	818
V	109 Dk. Willow Green	367
3	26 Nile Green	966
X	51-C Gold Brown	436
⟋	38 Dk. Orange	741
T	245 Atlantic Blue	799
S	253 Daffodil	444
·	61 Ecru	822
□	Cloth as is	

Backstitch Key

Symbol	J. & P. Coats six-strand floss	or DMC six-strand
	Color	
⊞	122 Watermelon	961
	109 Dk. Willow Green	367
	81-A Colonial Brown	433

Area of Backstitch: *122 Watermelon*—Outline around hearts. *109 Dk. Willow Green*—Stems. *81-A Colonial Brown*—Flower filaments.

Purchase three skeins of 61 Ecru and two skeins of 51-C Gold Brown. Buy one skein of each remaining color.

Making the first cross-stitch: On each, measure 3 1/2" across from top left corner; measure downwards 3 3/4" from top left corner. Mark point where two measurements intersect. Start sewing at arrow.

In color page H.

Areas of special concern: Initials change. See letters #4. There are 38 spaces available for bride's two, possibly three, initials. Leave 3 spaces between initials. Start where "S" begins. Work details out on graph paper.

Other materials: Ivory cotton/polyester pillowcases for standard or queen pillows—30" wide × 20". Pink satin ribbon, double-faced, 5/8" wide—3 1/4 yards.

Finishing directions

1. Add 1 1/4" borders on all sides of each design. Mark with pins. Using knotted single strand of beige thread, hand-stitch these lines by following one row in aida and by weaving in and out cloth with 1" running stitches (Illus. 122). Check to see that resulting squares are exact same size.

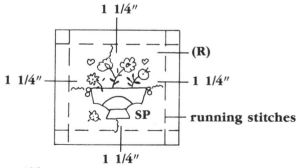

Illus. 122.

2. From running-stitch lines, add an additional 1/2″ seam allowance on all sides. Cut off excess fabric (Illus. 123).

3. On both designs, press back sides on running-stitch lines; press back top and bottom in same manner.

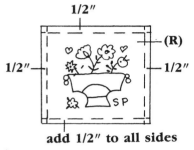

Illus. 123.

4. With right sides up, center one square over one case (my side borders are about 7 1/4″ and my top and bottom borders are about 4 1/4″). Pin. Baste. Machine-stitch 1/8″ from folded edges of design, pivoting at corners (Illus. 124).

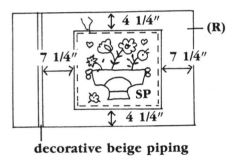

Illus. 124.

5. Cut ribbon in half. Center it over stitched edges of aida. Start in middle of inner side of pillowcase. At corners twist ribbon at right angles, and proceed in new direction (Illus. 125). Lap ribbon at end, and press back 1/4″. Baste. Machine-stitch close to edges of ribbon (Illus. 126).

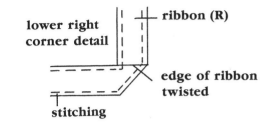

Illus. 125. Lower right corner detail.

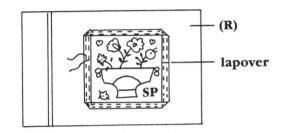

Illus. 126.

Illus. 127. Charted graph.

Illus. 127. (cont.).

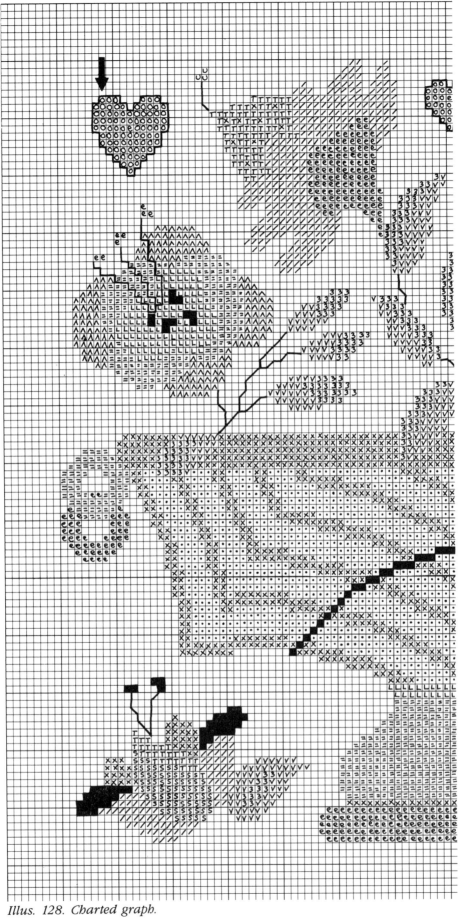

Illus. 128. Charted graph.

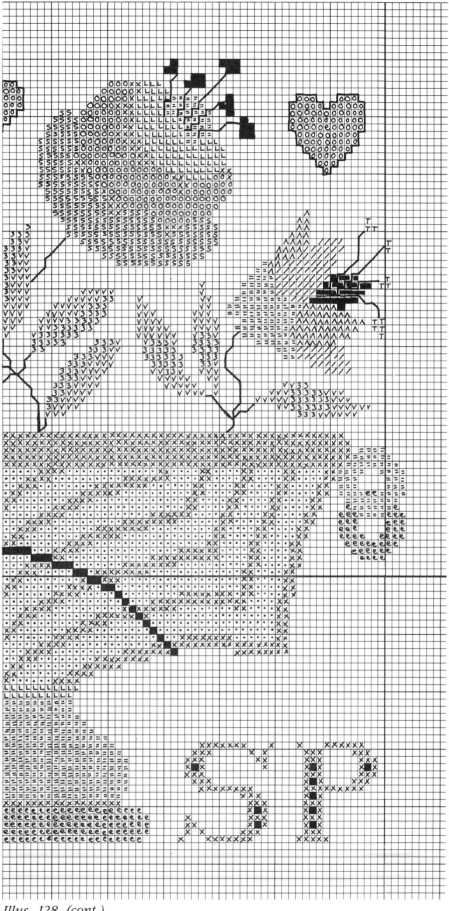

Illus. 128. (cont.).

Wedding Sampler

Degree of work: expert
Fabric: aida 11, ivory
Cut size of cloth needed: 23 1/2" wide × 23"
Finished size: approximately 18 1/4" wide ×
18 3/8"

In color page A.

Cross-Stitch Key

Symbol	J. & P. Coats six-strand floss Color	or DMC six-strand
⊠	132-A Parakeet*	996*
■	76 China Blue	825
U	253 Daffodil	444
S	235 Mint Gold	783
Z	1 White	Snow-White
L	100 Fast Red	816
◸	140 Signal Red	321
≡	59-B Dk. Rose	899
e	65 Beauty Pink	776
•	226 Pearl Pink	963
o	216 Avocado	469
2	28 Myrtle	700
◆	98 Fern Green	989
T	81-A Colonial Brown	433
3	62 Russet	435
▮	81-B Dk. Colonial Brown	801
☐	Cloth as is	

*On the lacy turquoise floral repeats, use one strand of floss for all cross- and backstitching. The other turquoise areas use the prescribed two strands.

Backstitch Key

Symbol	J. & P. Coats six-strand floss Color	or DMC six-strand
⌐	81-B Dk. Colonial Brown	801
	81-A Colonial Brown	433
	132-A Parakeet*	996*

Area of Backstitch: *81-B Dk. Colonial Brown*—Bird legs. *81-A Colonial Brown*—Center of each flower. *132-A Parakeet*—Within turquoise floral repeats.

Purchase three skeins of 132-A Parakeet. Purchase two skeins each of 140 Signal Red, 59-B Dk. Rose, and 216 Avocado. Buy one skein of each remaining color.

Making the first cross-stitch: Measure across 4 1/4" from top left corner; measure downwards 3" from top left corner. Mark point where two measurements intersect. Start sewing at arrow.

Areas of special concern: Wedding date and names change. See letters #1 and numbers #1. On line one, there are 91 spaces available for date but allow at least 3 spaces at beginning and 3 spaces at end as a border. Include word "on" if space permits. On line two, 87 spaces are available for bride's first name and word "and." Include middle initial or name if space permits. On line three, 75 spaces are available for groom's first and last name. Include middle initial if space permits. Line four remains as is. Leave 7 spaces between words, between month and day, and between day and year (ignore comma). Leave one space between each letter within word and between each number within date. Center each line. Work details out on graph paper.

Finishing directions: see "Mounting and Framing."

Margin to be added at mounting: add 15/16" borders.

Illus. 129. Charted graph.

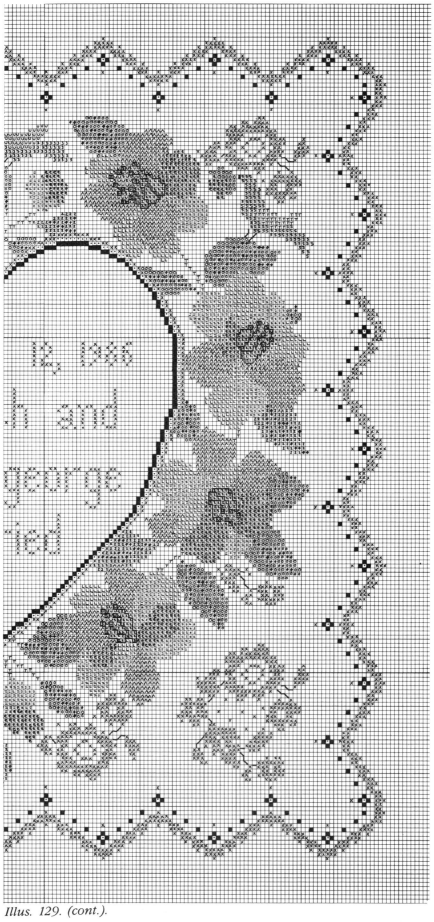

Illus. 129. (cont.).

Words of Love

Love Bears All Things

Quote: *The Holy Bible. 1 Corinthians 13:7*
Degree of work: *advanced*
Fabric: *cork linen, 19-thread count, cream*
Cut size of cloth needed: *19 1/2" wide × 20"*
Finished size: *approximately 15 1/4" wide ×*
16 1/4"

Cross-Stitch Key

Symbol	J. & P. Coats six-strand floss — Color	or DMC six-strand
⊠	*Use DMC color*	*444*
⊙	*Use DMC color*	*307*
▲	*Use DMC color*	*642*
•	*98 Fern Green*	*989*
■	*Use DMC color*	*727*
3	*62 Russet*	*435*
M	*81-B Dk. Colonial Brown*	*801*
U	*Use DMC color*	*676*
Z	*28 Myrtle*	*700*
╱	*1 White*	*Snow-White*
=	*213 Beige*	*644*
C	*Use DMC color*	*729*
S	*99 Grass Green*	*703*
☐	*Cloth as is*	

In color page F.

Backstitch Key

Symbol	J. & P. Coats six-strand floss — Color	or DMC six-strand
⊞	*Use DMC color*	*642*
	62 Russet	*435*
	Use DMC color	*444*
	28 Myrtle	*700*
	99 Grass Green	*703*
	98 Fern Green	*989*

Making the first cross-stitch: Measure across 3" from top left corner; measure downwards 3" from top left corner. Mark point where two measurements intersect. Start sewing at arrow.

Finishing directions: See "Mounting and Framing."

Margin to be added at mounting: Add 1 1/4" borders.

Area of Backstitch: *DMC 642*—Petal outlines on all daffodils. *62 Russet*—Trumpet outline on all daffodils. *DMC 444*—Veins on grass green leaves. *28 Myrtle*—Veins on light green leaves. *99 Grass Green*—Tips on grass green leaves. *98 Fern Green*—Tips on light green leaves.

Purchase two skeins each of DMC 444 and DMC 729. Buy one skein of each remaining color.

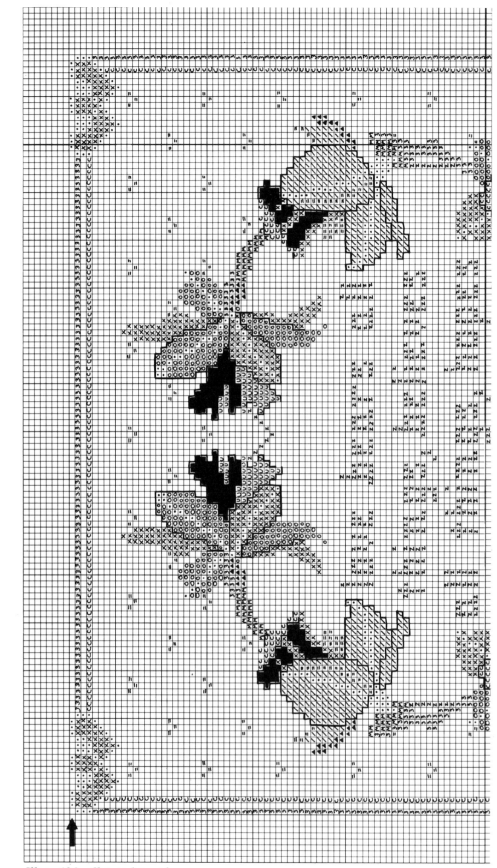

Illus. 130. Charted graph.

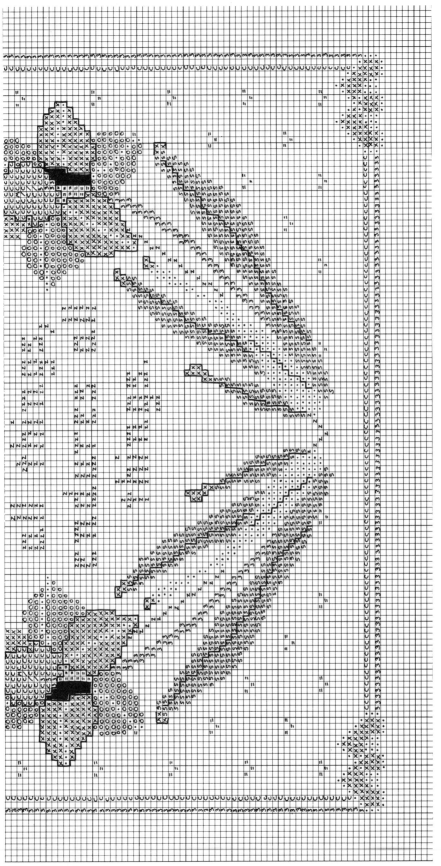

Illus. 130. (cont.).

Love Never Ends

Quote: The Holy Bible. 1 Corinthians 13:8
Degree of work: advanced
Fabric: aida 11, white
Cut size of cloth needed: 18" wide × 24"
*Finished size: approximately 13 3/4" wide ×
19 1/4"*

Cross-Stitch Key

Symbol	Color	J. & P. Coats six-strand floss	or DMC six-strand
■	12 Black		310
O	140 Signal Red		321
X	Use DMC color		414
△	24-A Oriental Blue		518
e	1 White		Snow-White
=	5-A Chartreuse		704
s	28 Myrtle		700
3	38 Dk. Orange		741
T	75-A Tropic Orange		920
·	90-A Bright Gold		783
c	91 Emerald Green		913
◆	Use DMC color		917
⧄	32 Purple		552
M	143 Lt. Cardinal		815
☐	Cloth as is		

Backstitch Key

Symbol	Color	J. & P. Coats six-strand floss	or DMC six-strand
⊞	12 Black		310

Area of Backstitch: *12 Black*—All.

*Purchase four skeins of DMC 414 and two skeins each
of 12 Black and 140 Signal Red. Buy one skein of each
remaining color.*

In color page C.

Making the first cross-stitch: Measure across
3 1/4" from top left corner; measure downwards
3" from top left corner. Mark point where two
measurements intersect. Start sewing at arrow.

Finishing directions: See "Mounting and
Framing."

Margin to be added at mounting: Add 1 1/8"
borders.

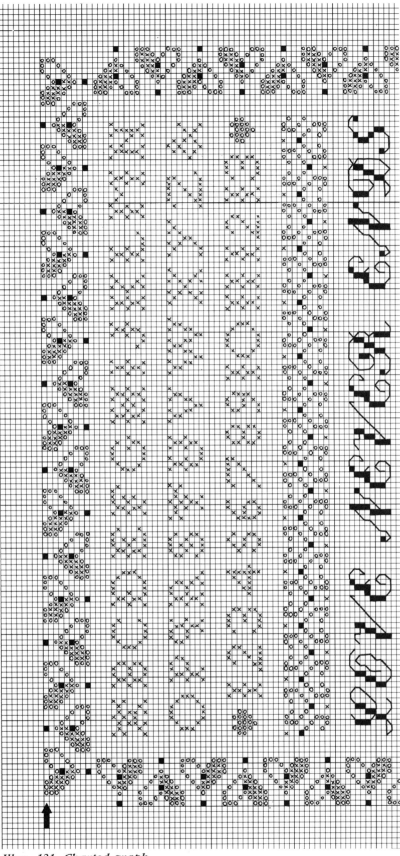

Illus. 131. Charted graph.

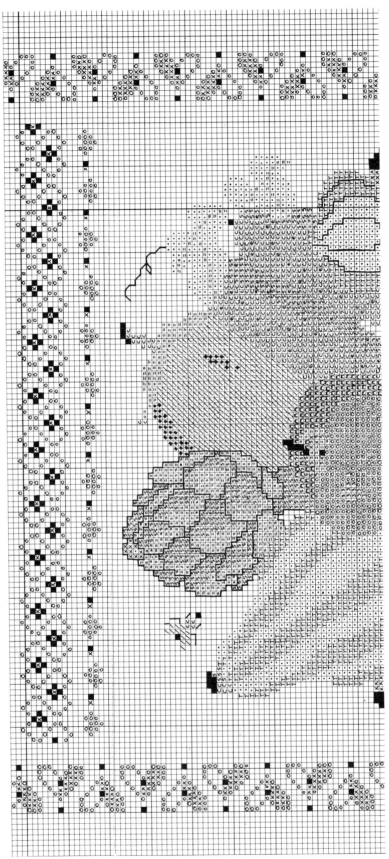

Illus. 131. (cont.).

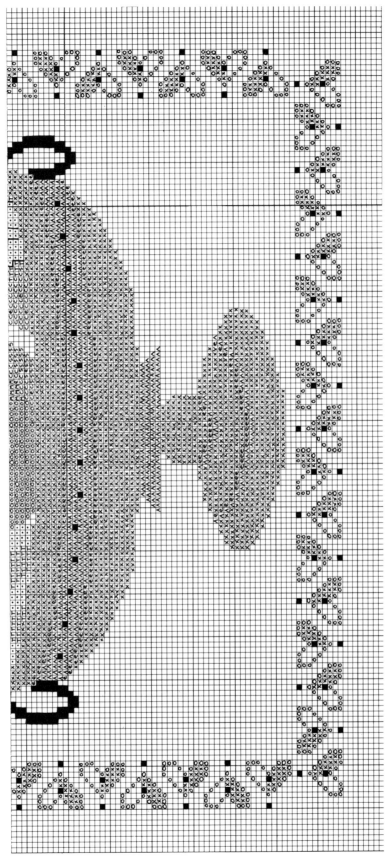

Illus. 131. (cont.).

Romeo and Juliet

Quote: Romeo and Juliet. *William Shakespeare*
Degree of work: advanced
Fabric: aida 11, white
Cut size of cloth needed: 24" wide × 22"
*Finished size: approximately 19 1/8" wide ×
17 1/8"*

Cross-Stitch Key

	J. & P. Coats six-strand floss	or DMC six-strand
Symbol	**Color**	
⊠	76 China Blue	825
③	120 Crimson	351
⊙	69 Lt. Steel Blue	809
⊟	12 Black	310
◁	81-A Colonial Brown	433
·	260 Maple Wood	437
e	Use DMC color	642
■	11 Orange	972
☐	Cloth as is	

Backstitch Key

	J. & P. Coats six-strand floss	or DMC six-strand
Symbol	**Color**	
⊞	81-A Colonial Brown	433
	120 Crimson	351
	12 Black	310

Area of Backstitch: *81-A Colonial Brown—*Two crosses
on boat and line in center of biggest sail. *120 Crimson—*
Vertical line in bottom of boat. *12 Black—*All rigging.

*Purchase four skeins of 69 Lt. Steel Blue and three
skeins each of 76 China Blue and 120 Crimson. Buy two
skeins of DMC 642. Buy one skein of each remaining
color.*

In color page B.

Making the first cross-stitch: Measure across
3 3/4" from top left corner; measure downwards
3 3/4" from top left corner. Mark point where two
measurements intersect. Start sewing at arrow.

Finishing directions: See "Mounting and
Framing."

Margin to be added at mounting: Add 3/4"
borders. Measure from outer edge light blue oc-
tagons.

Illus. 132. Charted graph.

Illus. 132. (cont.).

Our Love Should Not Be Just Words and Talk

Quote: The Holy Bible. 1 John 3:18
Degree of work: expert
Fabric: aida 11, ivory
Cut size of cloth needed: 24" wide × 20"
Finished size: approximately 18 7/8" wide × 15 5/8"

In color page H.

Cross-Stitch Key

Symbol	J. & P. Coats six-strand floss Color	or DMC six-strand
☒	81 Dk. Brown	434
e	143 Lt. Cardinal	815
U	140 Signal Red	321
■	75-A Tropic Orange	920
◹	12 Black	310
Q	90-A Bright Gold	783
◩	5-A Chartreuse	704
O	99 Grass Green	703
S	109 Dk. Willow Green	367
•	215 Apple Green	471
M	81-B Dk. Colonial Brown	801
T	267 Lt. Salmon	754
3	1 White	Snow-White
=	69 Lt. Steel Blue	809
L	Use DMC color	414
☐	Cloth as is	

Making the first cross-stitch: Measure across 3" from top left corner; measure downwards 3 3/8" from top left corner. Mark point where two measurements intersect. Start sewing at arrow.

Finishing directions: See "Mounting and Framing."

Margin to be added at mounting: Add 1" borders.

Backstitch Key

Symbol	J. & P. Coats six-strand floss Color	or DMC six-strand
⊞	69 Lt. Steel Blue	809
	81-B Dk. Colonial Brown	801
	12 Black	310

Area of Backstitch: *69 Lt. Steel Blue*—All clouds; outline on bottom of birds in top left corner and lower right corner; outline at throat of bird in lower left corner. *81-B Dk. Colonial Brown*—All leaf and cherry stems; outline around red-eyed birds. *12 Black*—All bird legs and feather details; outline around blue-eyed birds.

Purchase three skeins of 5-A Chartreuse and two skeins each of 81 Dk. Brown, 99 Grass Green, 109 Dk. Willow Green, and 215 Apple Green. Buy one skein of each remaining color.

Illus. 133. Charted graph.

Illus. 133. (cont.).

Love Conquers All

Quote: Eclogues. *Virgil*
Degree of work: expert
Fabric: aida 11, white
Cut size of cloth needed: 21" wide × 20"
Finished size: approximately 16 7/8" wide × 15 1/2"

In color page E.

Cross-Stitch Key

Symbol	J. & P. Coats six-strand floss		or DMC six-strand
		Color	
⧄	122	Watermelon	961
•	12	Black	310
=	143	Lt. Cardinal	815
◿	132-A	Parakeet	996
S	32	Purple	552
U	8	Blue	775
O	223	Sun Gold	743
☐		Cloth as is	

Purchase five skeins each of 122 Watermelon and 223 Sun Gold. Purchase three skeins each of 143 Lt. Cardinal and 132-A Parakeet and two skeins of 32 Purple. Buy one skein of each remaining color.

Making the first cross-stitch: Measure across 3" from top left corner; measure downwards 3" from top left corner. Mark point where two measurements intersect. Start sewing at arrow.

Finishing directions: See "Mounting and Framing."

Margin to be added at mounting: Add 1 1/8" borders.

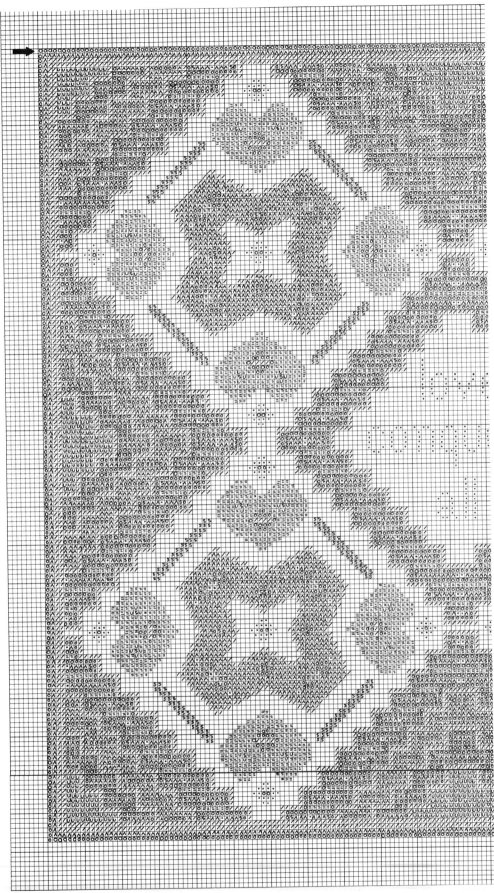

Illus. 134. Charted graph.

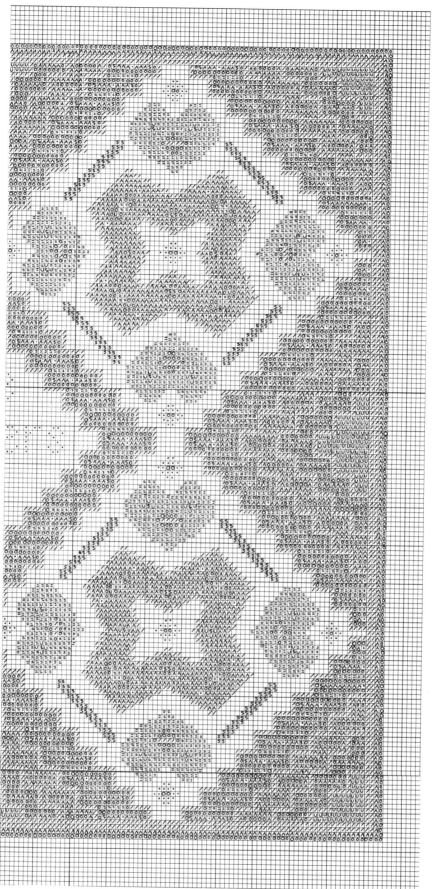

Illus. 134. (cont.).

116

All Hearts in Love

Quote: Much Ado about Nothing. *William Shakespeare*
Degree of work: expert
Fabric: cork linen, 19-thread count, pink
Cut size of cloth needed: 30" wide × 22"
Finished size: approximately 25 3/8" wide × 16 1/2"

In color page A.

Cross-Stitch Key

Symbol	J. & P. Coats six-strand floss	or DMC six-strand
	Color	
⊠	122 Watermelon	961
△	1 White	Snow-White
⊙	223 Sun Gold	743
⊟	201 Aquatone	964
•	65 Beauty Pink	776
⊘	235 Mint Gold	783
⋃	62 Russet	435
③	222 Dk. Aquatone	958
■	81-B Dk. Colonial Brown	801
⊤	8 Blue	775
◆	143 Lt. Cardinal	815
⧄	37 Dk. Lavender	554
⑤	32 Purple	552
☐	Cloth as is	

Making the first cross-stitch: Measure across 3" from top left corner; measure downwards 3 1/4" from top left corner. Mark point where two measurements intersect. Start sewing at arrow.

Finishing directions: See "Mounting and Framing."

Margin to be added at mounting: Add 1" borders.

Backstitch Key

Symbol	J. & P. Coats six-strand floss	or DMC six-strand
	Color	
⊞	81-B Dk. Colonial Brown	801

Area of Backstitch: *81-B Dk. Colonial Brown*—Details in all flowers and leaves.

Purchase five skeins of 65 Beauty Pink and three skeins each of 1 White, 223 Sun Gold, 201 Aquatone, and 235 Mint Gold. Purchase two skeins each of 122 Watermelon, 62 Russet, 222 Dk. Aquatone, and 37 Dk. Lavender. Buy one skein of each remaining color.

Illus. 135. Charted graph.

Illus. 135. (cont.).

119

Teach Me To Love

In color page D.

Quote: paraphrase from Evening Hymn. *Bishop Thomas Ken*
Degree of work: expert
Fabric: aida 11, white
Cut size of cloth needed: 30" wide × 22"
Finished size: approximately 24 1/4" wide × 16 3/8"

Cross-Stitch Key

Symbol	J. & P. Coats six-strand floss	or DMC six-strand
	Color	
⊠	245 Atlantic Blue	799
Ⓞ	218 Coral Glow	893
Ⓣ	71 Pewter Grey	415
⊟	223 Sun Gold	743
Ⓢ	32 Purple	552
③	8 Blue	800
·	215 Apple Green	471
◩	109 Dk. Willow Green	367
■	12 Black	310
⧄	143 Lt. Cardinal	815
☐	Cloth as is	

Making the first cross-stitch: Measure across 3" from top left corner; measure downwards 3" from top left corner. Mark point where two measurements intersect. Start sewing at arrow.

Finishing directions: See "Mounting and Framing."

Margin to be added at mounting: Add 3/4" borders.

Backstitch Key

Symbol	J. & P. Coats six-strand floss	or DMC six-strand
	Color	
⊞	109 Dk. Willow Green	367

Area of Backstitch: *109 Dk. Willow Green—All.*

Purchase four skeins of 109 Dk. Willow Green and three skeins each of 245 Atlantic Blue, 218 Coral Glow, and 223 Sun Gold. Purchase two skeins each of 32 Purple, 8 Blue, 215 Apple Green, and 143 Lt. Cardinal. Buy one skein of each remaining color.

Illus. 136. Charted graph.

Illus. 136. (cont.).

Alphabets and Numerals

1. Six Squares High—Lower Case

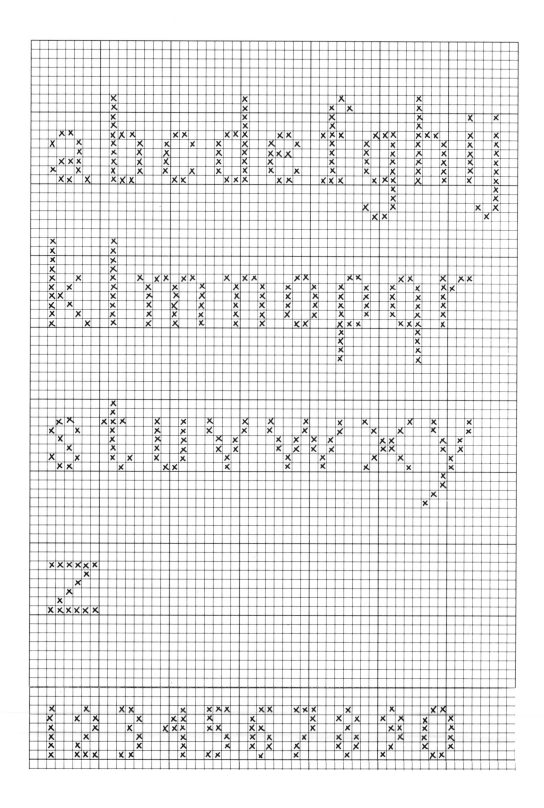

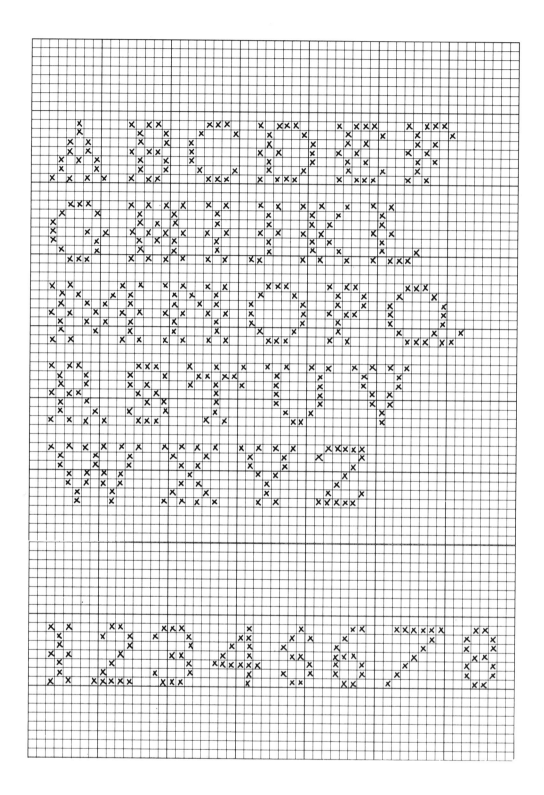

3. Nine Squares High—Upper Case

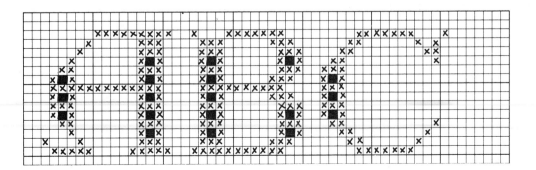

4. Fourteen Squares High—Upper Case with Second Color

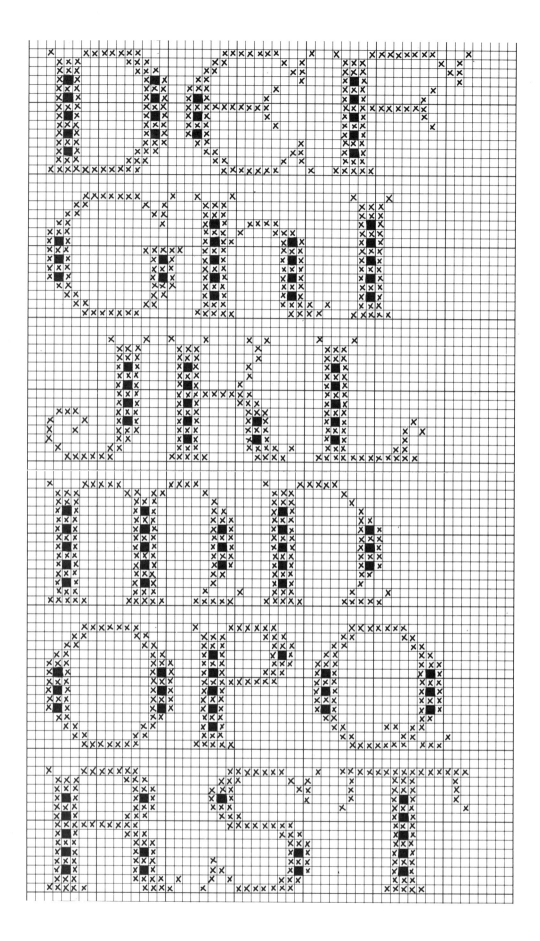

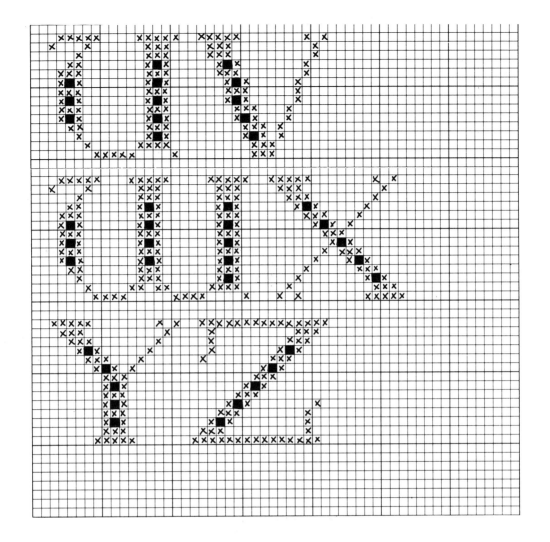

Index